First Hand Faith

RECAPTURE A PASSIONATE
LOVE FOR THE SAVIOR

Bruce H. Wilkinson

MULTNOMAH BOOKS
SISTERS, OREGON

FIRST HAND FAITH
© 1996 by Bruce Wilkinson and Chip MacGregor

published by Multnomah Books
a part of the Questar publishing family

International Standard Book Number: 1–88530–537–0

Printed in the United States of America

For information:
QUESTAR PUBLISHERS, INC.
POST OFFICE BOX 1720
SISTERS, OREGON 97759

97 98 99 00 01 02 03 — 08 07 06 05 04 03 02

DEDICATION

One of the delights of authorship is the privilege of this page. It's so important to all of us who write that it always precedes all that is written. Why? Because most frequently, that which follows wouldn't have been written had it not been without the influence and contribution of that person(s).

Often the selection can be difficult because so many have had an influence that they all appear to be relatively equal. In the case of *First Hand Faith*, however, the selection was immediate upon the question I asked myself: "Who is the one person I know who sits in the 'First Chair' as a way of life as well as enabling me the most to pursue that 'First Chair' throughout my own pilgrimage?" Instantly, I knew the answer, because there is one person, for more than twenty-five years, whose life continues to be a model to me of holiness and passion for the Lord Jesus Christ—one person whose life continues to be an inspiration and deep encouragement to me in the process of becoming more of a true disciple of Jesus Christ. Without this person and their love, prayers and support, this book could never have been written because I couldn't have written it. I wouldn't have known of the truth, nor even have paid the price to become acquainted with the truth as poured out through my own life. So it gives me unique and great pleasure to dedicate First Hand Faith—to my fellow pilgrim, soulmate, closest friend, and spiritual warrior, Darlene M. Wilkinson, my wife.

ACKNOWLEDGEMENTS

Three people receive great credit for this book—one in the conception and pregnancy stage, and two in the delivery process. Without my good friend John Van Diest, this book would only have remained a series of sermons, audio tapes, and video tape series. For more than twenty years John has been encouraging, exhorting, prodding, and praying. Without his faith and loyalty, this book would never have progressed past his dream. Thanks, strong-hearted John—may your heart rejoice in this trophy of your ministry in my life.

Then my diligent assistant at Walk Thru the Bible Ministries, Dianne Agee, who took my rough chapters via e-mail and brought her excellent touch to the manuscript. Thanks, Dianne, for not only being such a wonderful assistant, but a fellow servant of the Lord. Lastly, however, Chip MacGregor has brought the finesse, cohesion and completeness that only the most gifted of editors is able to do. A true wordsmith. Although I brought the ingredients to the table in a large mixing bowl, it wasn't until Chip rolled up his sleeves that my rough manuscript was literally transformed into a book. Thanks, Chip, for your excellence, diligence, and creativity. May your heart also rejoice in this joint-effort to serve the Lord.

TABLE OF CONTENTS

SECTION A: UNDERSTANDING THE THREE CHAIRS

Chapter 1 —The Three Chairs — 9

Chapter 2 —Your Work and Your Family — 25

Chapter 3 —The Role of the Church — 43

SECTION B: DEVELOPING FIRST HAND FAITH

Chapter 4 — Commitment, Compromise, and Conflict — 59

Chapter 5 —From Compromise to Commitment — 77

Chapter 6 —The Secrets of the Committed, Part One — 91

Chapter 7 —The Secrets of the Committed, Part Two — 111

Chapter 8 —People, Possessions, and Purposelessness — 125

Chapter 9 —From Possessions to People — 145

SECTION C: LEAVING A LEGACY

Chapter 10 — Raising Godly Children — 161

Chapter 11 — The First Chair Father — 187

Chapter 12 — The First Chair Mother — 209

Chapter 13 — Next Generation Thinking — 227

Understanding
the
Three Chairs

CHAPTER ONE

The Three Chairs

"Do you know who that is?" the man next to me at the conference asked, pointing to a young man on the other side of the auditorium. "That's Rob, the son of that famous Christian leader!" Then he named a man whom I had respected all my life, an internationally known speaker. The first thought that came to my mind was, "I want to talk with him. I'd really like to find out what it was like to grow up in such a godly home as that."

During the next break I made my way over to that young man and introduced myself.

"I'm Bruce Wilkinson," I said, smiling. "I've been an admirer of your father for years. I'd love to know what it was like growing up in your dad's home."

That young man's mouth fell open. He stared at me with cold eyes for a moment, as if trying to get his emotions under control. Finally, he squeezed out, "I hate my father. I hate God." Then he swore a blue streak, muttered, "Stay away from me," and stalked out of the room.

You could have picked my jaw up from off the floor. I was stunned the son of one of the most famous Christian leaders had just cursed God and said that he hated his father! How on earth could that happen? How did he get to that point? As I pondered it, my thoughts soon turned to my own family. I couldn't think of anything worse than somebody walking up to one of my kids, asking if they were the son or daughter of Bruce Wilkinson, and being sworn at for mentioning my name. My children rejecting the Lord I love and serve? How could I keep that from happening?

That conference meeting took place more than twenty-five years ago, and I still remember it as though it were yesterday. The pain and hatred in that young man's eyes still grieves me. The catastrophic failure of his father still haunts me. Whatever the secrets were to keeping that from happening in my own life, marriage, and family, to keep from passing on such a life failure, I was committed to finding and using. What can we do to ensure that our faith abides and flourishes in the next generation?

All too often, the church doesn't seem to know what to do about this urgent problem. Christians don't want anyone to know their kids' faith is failing. Too many Christians sweep these problems under the rug. Some even place the piano over the rug to make sure nobody notices! They act as if putting this crisis out of sight will make it disappear. It's not disappearing, though; it's multiplying at an alarming rate.

THE THREE GENERATION PRINCIPLE

Scripture reveals the solution to this crucial issue of passing on our faith, and it paves the way for us to understand what things change from one generation to the next. More importantly, the Bible shows us what we can do about it. As you read this chapter, you will begin to understand how we all live in different "generations." Which one you are in determines a great deal about your entire life.

Imagine for a moment that you are at a family reunion. Three generations gather together to celebrate the 50th wedding anniversary of your parents. Your folks have a few health concerns, but no aches or pains are going to dampen this milestone. Married to the same woman for 50 years, your dad still teases his bride as if she were that 15-year-old he met on the nearby farm. Then there's your generation, everyone in middle age, and a couple of your siblings ribbing you because you are nearing 48 and the half century mark is only a couple of short years away. You glance around at your children, spanning the teens and early twenties. One just got married last year.

Those three generations are marked not only by age, but by culture and life values. How different is your generation from your parents', and your children seem to live in a world that is far different from your own. When your parents were born in the 1920's, there were no televisions or airline travel. Few people had a car, so many had never traveled more than 100 miles from the places of their birth. Entertainment didn't dominate their lives because library books and an occasional movie were the primary sources for filling up the limited free time. They lived a simpler, though harder, lifestyle.

Your generation brought with it changes, but you weren't raised with shopping malls, computers, or portable phones like your children were. Television changed our lives, everyone began going to college, and the space race gave our generation visions of grandeur. You were raised on *I Love Lucy* and *Father Knows Best*, Saturday afternoon baseball, and portable transistor radios.

Now, your children watch MTV, *NYPD Blue*, and HBO. They listen to their own CD players, converse with total strangers on the internet, and spend their free time at shopping malls or playing games on CD-ROM. You wonder, in the quiet moments in late evening, if all this "progress" has been in the right direction. Technology has literally exploded and, though you're not sure, it appears that many people are exploding with it. With the rise of rock-n-roll came the release of sexual boundaries, and all the liberalizing of morality has degraded culture, destroyed lives with drugs, and demeaned our country's commitment to Christ.

Just yesterday you read on the USA Today front page that 60 percent of all couples getting married today will divorce. Sixty percent! Your parents remarked the other day that only one of their friends got divorced. About 25 percent of your friends have split.

Your children have less than a 50 percent chance of a successful marriage. Is that progress? Or is it a drift away from God? It's different generations, to be sure, and astounding differences economically, physically, socially, morally, and spiritually.

But these are really surface issues, fruit born from hidden roots. In this book I want to take the cover off another set of generational differences and reveal what has been going on beneath the surface. The Bible has profound answers to the painful and distressing issue of generational drift. It offers answers for all people, for all time, regardless of when they lived, where they lived, or what they lived for. The Bible even has wisdom for those wondering why they lived in the first place! These generational insights from the pages of Scripture are universal truths. They exist for all time and to all people. They are supra-cultural, supra-national, and supra-gender. Because the truth is with us all, this truth is for your life, too.

In order to serve you better, I have presented what the Bible teaches through the parable of "Three Chairs," representing the three different types of people in the world. These categories are remarkable. Whenever I have spoken about these Three Chairs, the results have been astounding. We quickly and intuitively see that they make incredible sense. The biblical concepts have immediate power. When you understand how life works in each of these Three Chairs for yourself, your children, and your grandchildren, you will find incredible internal motivation to make changes. That motivation won't be out of guilt or defeat, but out of an immediate desire for your good. You'll finally know you have the real answers. No one will have to convince you. Your conscience and common sense will clearly confirm it to you.

If you are like most of the thousands who have examined these principles, you will feel liberated. It will be like someone walked you out of the murky darkness and brought you into the light. Things that you previously bumped into, that caused confusion and despair, or that frustrated you beyond words—they'll now be clear to you. Rarely has anyone heard me present these powerful, transforming truths and had to seek me out later to ask what to do. Once they know the truth, they know exactly what to do.

You will also know what to do. You will see with such new-found clarity that the answers and action steps will be obvious to you. Your heart will sing. You will be released because you finally understand how you can impact the next generation with the truth. As Jesus said, "The truth will set you free."

As you turn these pages and your perceptions grow about yourself and your life, you will become aware that these very same principles govern not only individuals, but all types of organizations. Everything that people are involved with in life is touched by these truths— churches, businesses, even nations. Not only will you know where all of your family and friends fit in the three-part pattern of life, you will know where your church fits, and where your business fits.

THE THREE CHAIRS

In order to make these issues more visual and practical, I have used three different chairs to represent three different generations. Picture three chairs in your mind: the First Chair is the one on your left side, the Second Chair is in the middle, and the Third Chair sits on the right. By the time you are finished reading this chapter, you will know where you sit, where your parents sit, and where your children sit. Let me introduce you to the Three Chairs and how I discovered them.

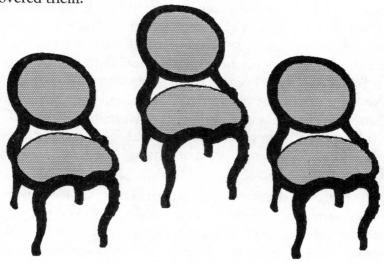

After that shattering conversation with the son of the Christian leader, I began to search for an answer to the problem of passing on my faith. My antennae were out, and I was struck over and over again how a downhill slide was apparent in so many areas of life. Churches that began as Gospel-preaching churches began in time to slide toward simply being social gatherings. Colleges that began as places to train men for the ministry began to slide toward liberal academic platforms for anti-God spokesmen. Nearly everywhere I looked in life, even in history, there was an unmistakable downhill slide away from God. That which started in such vibrant faith and resolute commitment ended generations later in empty faith, continuing conflict, and even atheistic antagonism toward God.

Many churches are birthed as dynamic powerhouses for God, impacting their societies in dramatic ways for the redemption of the people and cultures of which they are a part. The Bible is preached openly as the Word of God and every person is seen as in need of eternal salvation. But as time goes on, the wisdom of God becomes less important and the wisdom of man takes preeminence.

I'll never forget more than twenty years ago being invited to speak on a Sunday morning at one of America's most outstanding churches, a body that influenced not only its entire city, but also the whole country. How honored I felt, standing in that pulpit and recounting a bit of their history. But when I said, "Please open your Bibles to the passage of the day," I noticed that no one moved. That's when the principle of the Three Chairs hit me. As I later discovered over lunch, this congregation didn't bother to bring their Bibles to church because the pastor preached more out of *Time* or *Newsweek* than out of Matthew, Mark, Luke, or John. His congregation did not believe even the most basics tenets of the Gospel. For the most part, they were unconverted. They gathered more for music and social interaction. The entire church had moved from godliness to godlessness.

Years ago on the American Atlantic coast, villages began creating life-saving stations for emergencies at sea. The people would gather for training, prepared in case a ship ran aground. They had lifejackets and lifeboats at the ready, and moorages were soon built so that locals could keep their boats close at hand. Over time, the gathering of people became more important, and the talk of saving lives was less so. Eventually, these gatherings became private clubs, which had no interest at all in being bothered with talking about saving lives. In some cases, those who insisted on saving lives at sea were asked to leave, so that the others could focus on what interested them most — boating and parties. Many of the yacht clubs of the upper Atlantic coast got started just this way. Instead of saving the lives of others, they now focus on meeting their own needs for socializing. That's an apt illustration for many churches today. Founded with the idea of saving lives, they have now rejected the notion of salvation and focus on themselves.

The First Chair in our metaphor is the godly chair, and those who sit in it remain close to Him. The Third Chair is the godless chair, and those who sit in it have rejected God. They have moved away from Him, so as to focus on themselves. *From godliness to godlessness.* That's the general movement of history.

"Godless?" you ask. Yes, for they were without God. They did not know Him. They were wonderful people, but as far as heaven was concerned, they were godless.

When all of this flooded into my mind that Sunday morning as I stumbled through reading six or seven verses, I could only ask the question, "What on earth happened?" How could a vibrant church body grow so distant from the Lord? The Principle of the Three Chairs explains it, and it strikes home in nearly every situation I have experienced.

But the good news is that the trend is reversible! In fact, the trend is reversing all across the country and in many nations of the world, and there are times all through history when that is true. Those who were far away from God are being brought near. The godless are embracing God. Why? Because God is the ultimate trend-reverser. His Word discloses the secrets of the ages for all who would but seek.

As I mentioned, I was a seeker, looking for a method of prevention. And I also knew first-hand that the Bible is the absolute Truth for life. So, with a careful eye, I began to scour the books of the Bible one by one, seeking the key that would unlock the door of insight, set me free, and liberate my marriage and, ultimately, my children. As it always is, the Lord rewards those who fervently seek Him. My reward? His answer to my penetrating question.

I first saw it when I wasn't even thinking about it. I was just reading the Bible and there it was—obvious, *because three generations were described in only a few verses.* They were right next to each other. It starts in the last chapter of the book of Joshua (24:1-33) and continues into the book of Judges (1:1-2:13):

First Chair	Second Chair	Third Chair
Chair on Left	Chair in Middle	Chair on Right
Joshua 24:1-15 and Judges 2:7a, 8-9	Joshua 24:16-31 and Judges 1:1-2;7b	Judges 2:10-23

THE FIRST CHAIR:
THE LIFE OF JOSHUA

There's no doubt about it. Joshua is a primary example of a person who sits in the First Chair. He knows the Lord and lives his life to serve Him. Every time you see Joshua in the pages of the Bible, you find him seeking to please God in his faith and actions.

Joshua once said to his people, "Now therefore, fear the Lord, serve Him in sincerity and in truth, and put away the gods which your fathers served on the other side of the River and in Egypt. Serve the Lord! *But as for me and my house, we will serve the Lord*" (Joshua 24:14, 15c).

Can you see why Joshua is in the First Chair? He loves the Lord. He has a heart for God. He even commits his family to serving the Lord. Joshua has first-hand faith. This is a man totally devoted to God — that's what it's like in the First Chair. The people of Joshua's generation were also committed to God. They had seen Him work mighty wonders; they knew God had been with them during the difficult times of taking the land. This generation had first-hand knowledge and experience of the God of the heavens at work in their midst. That's the mark of people in the First Chair. They know God first-hand, love Him, and they've seen Him work in their lives. They can pass on the good news of Jesus Christ because they have experienced His mighty power in their own lives.

THE SECOND CHAIR:
THE ELDERS WHO OUTLIVED JOSHUA

Let's trace what happened to Joshua's descendants and the generation that outlived him. Read Joshua 24:31 and Judges 2:7b and watch for the two key signs of that second generation:

Joshua 24:31: *"Israel served the Lord* all the days of Joshua, and all the days of the elders who outlived Joshua, *who had known all the works of the Lord* which He had done for Israel."

Judges 2:7: "So the *people served the Lord* all the days of Joshua, and all the days of the elders who outlived Joshua, *who had seen all the great works of the Lord* which He had done for Israel."

The child who is raised in a First Chair family is most fortunate. He sees with his own eyes the commitment of his parents and how God actually answered the specific prayers of his parents. It was the same in Joshua's day. The second generation received the innumerable benefits of their parents' first-hand faith–they had *"known all the works of the Lord* which He had done for Israel."

This generation that came after Joshua still believed in the Lord, but there was one significant difference: their faith wasn't original. They hadn't dealt personally with the Lord. Instead, they relied on the faith of their parents and the stories of what God had done in their parent's generation. That alone had been enough to develop faith in God. As children, they either saw the miracles of

God's intervention on their parents' behalf, or found out about the Lord's miracles from their fathers and mothers. They heard how God had parted the waters of the Red Sea, brought water from a rock, and provided manna in the wilderness. They believed the stories, but they were a generation removed from actually having dealt with the issues personally. Their parents were the adults who marched around the walls of Jericho, while they themselves only heard about God's miracle in that battle. They believed all the facts *about* God, though they didn't experience Him personally. That's the Second Chair.

THE THIRD CHAIR: ANOTHER GENERATION AROSE AFTER THEM

You only have to turn a few pages in your Bible to read what happened when the second generation had children. Judges 2:10 tells the sad story:

> "When all that generation had been gathered to their fathers, another generation arose after them *who did not know the Lord* nor *the work which He had done* for Israel."

Do you see it? There are three profound differences between the second and third generations. First, the third generation *"did not know the Lord."* In other words, they did not know God personally and they were not saved. Tragic, isn't it? The grandchildren of Joshua's day didn't even count themselves as believers.

Second, the third generation *"did not know the work* which He (the Lord) had done for Israel." That's difficult to believe, that they didn't even know the stories of the great miracles their grandparents had experienced. They didn't know that the Jericho walls tumbled to the ground because the nation of Israel marched and blew trumpets, or that God parted the Jordan, or that the sun stood still. *They didn't even know. It's not that they rejected them; they didn't even know about them.* Why not?

There could be only one reason as I see it: their parents never told them. And why not? Think about it. The moment a father or mother would tell the story of God's great answers to prayer in their parent's life, the immediate question in the heart of the child would be, "Where are those great miracles in our lives?" When first-hand faith gets passed on, it always becomes, at that moment, second-hand faith. *And second-hand faith doesn't have any first-hand experiences.* You go through the motions, but there isn't any vibrant reality behind them. First-hand faith has experienced the reality of God; second-hand faith has only heard about it. By the time we get to third-hand faith—well, there's no faith left. The people of the third generation don't believe it because there is no reality for them to experience.

The First Chair person is saved.

The Second Chair person is saved.

The Third Chair person is not saved.

The First Chair person has the works of God.

The Second Chair person has heard about the works of God.

The Third Chair person doesn't know about the works of God.

What is the result, then, of this third-hand "unfaith"? Read the next few verses in Judges 2:

"Then the children of Israel *did evil in the sight of the Lord,* and s*erved the Baals*; and they *forsook the Lord God of their fathers....*"

The person sitting in the Third Chair *forsakes* the Lord God of their fathers.

The person in the Third Chair *does evil* in the sight of the Lord.

The person in the Third Chair *replaces* God with other gods.

No matter where you look in life or in history, this three-stage process holds true. For instance, consider the early days of the founding of America. In the beginning, there were people who had experienced God's miraculous work, and they brought revival to our nation. Followers of Christ believed the hand of God was present in the founding of our nation. The founding documents of our nation are replete with references to our Creator.

The first colleges in this country—Harvard, Princeton, William and Mary were all founded to train men to preach the Gospel. They were started by men and women who sat in the First Chair; who had experienced the providence of God. But, the following generation didn't have the same vital relationship with God, and they carried on those values out of tradition rather than conviction. They continued what the earlier generation had done because "that's they way we've been doing it," not from a resolute commitment to living life so that it fully pleases Jesus Christ. By the time the third generation arrived, any mention of "God" was a bit of an embarrassment. This third generation has remained in these institutions for the most part—out of tradition—and Ivy League students today have told me that even carrying a Bible into a classroom can get you mocked and scorned all too often.

Does that surprise you? It shouldn't, considering the pattern we've just seen in the book of Judges. As the Bible so forthrightly states, the third generation forsakes the God of their fathers, does evil, and serves other gods. What began as a training ground for the people of God has turned into a playroom for those who have rejected God. That's evidence of the generational drift that is at work in our world.

THE THREE CHAIRS IN YOUR LIVING ROOM

Now, let's bring these Three Chairs into your living room for a moment—because they are there, whether you've seen them or not. If you grew up in a home committed to Jesus Christ, you probably came to know Christ as your personal savior between the ages of 5 and 13. But you may not be nearly as committed to Him and His calling as your parents were, unless you already paid the price of becoming a First Chair believer. Most Christians today are Second Chair believers. They know all about the faith, but it's not vibrant to them. It doesn't significantly shape their values or their lifestyles. They can talk to their children about their walk with God in general terms, but they have no first-hand experience to pass on.

Unfortunately, those who remain in the Second Chair typically raise Third Chair children. These are the young adults who are leaving the church in untold numbers. Many of these children want no part in the kind of empty faith that they saw in their parents while growing up. In fact, they don't even know that there is such a thing as a First Chair follower of Jesus. They don't see how the Bible affects their lives, and they've got better things to do on Sunday morning than sit in church. So they reject God because they don't know Him.

THE CHAIR WITH YOUR NAME ON IT

Would you describe yourself as a believer in Jesus who is sold out to the Lord? Do you seek to love and serve Him with all your heart? Or would you describe yourself as a believer who has not been able to make Christ the center of his life? Or are you filled with uncertainty and internal conflicts about God and the real meaning of life?

Where do you sit? That's the real question. Do you sit in the First Chair, experiencing the presence of God and allowing Him to use you, shape you, and minister to others through you? Or do you sit in the Second Chair, believing the truth and appreciating what God is doing in the lives of others, but always wondering why you don't have the same spiritual passion as they do? Look at the overview of where we've gone so far and see if you can find the chair to which you've grown accustomed.

The First Generation	The Second Generation	The Third Generation
Joshua's Generation	*Elder's Generation*	*Another Generation*
Knows God	Knows God	Knows not God
Has the works	Knows about the works	Knows not the works
Serves the Lord	Serves the Lord of fathers	Serves false gods
First-Hand Faith	Second-Hand Faith	No Faith

In many ways, the generation you are in determines almost everything in your life: your values, your friends, your goals, and ultimately your eternity. Before discussing the answer to this problem, perhaps it would be helpful to see some of the primary characteristics of each generation, and the secret of transitioning to the First Chair–and staying there!

STUDY QUESTIONS

1. What marked Joshua's generation?

2. What was different about the second generation?

3. Why does the third generation end up rejecting the faith of the first?

4. How are your values and lifestyle choices different from that of your parents?

5. What chair are you sitting in right now?

CHAPTER TWO

Your Work and Your Family:

Two Key Differences Between the Chairs

Nearly everything in your life is a result of which Chair you sit in. Your choices don't determine which Chair you sit in; rather, it's the opposite. The Chair in which you sit determines the choices you will make.

The characteristics of each Chair are unique, and those who sit in each take on its characteristics. Therefore, the moment you discern which Chair a person sits in, you have a whole range of information about much of his life, his values, his goals, and even his family. The reverse is also true. When you meet a new person, the information you gather can tell you which Chair he is in. What you learn in this chapter will greatly heighten your discernment. The threads that weave the seat cushions on each of these chairs are of a distinct color and pattern. When you understand those distinct colors and patterns, you will know which Chair they sit in—no matter how they may arrange or decorate the Chair with their own personalities and unique situations.

Even though what you are about to learn gives you a window into the souls of others, it is, more importantly, a mirror into your own soul. You may start out thinking of people in your extended family or circle of friends as you read. But before you know it, your attention will turn to the person holding this book. Why? I believe the Holy Spirit shines the light of insight at full force as the powerful principles of the Three Chairs illuminate your life.

In this chapter, we will talk about two areas that clarify the differences between First Chair and Second Chair faith. In order to set the stage for the rest of the book, this chapter focuses on broad concepts. By the end it, you should be able to imagine yourself looking closely at each Chair, easily describing the whole landscape of a person's life who sits in each.

THE ROLE OF WORK IN THE THREE CHAIRS

If someone meeting you for the first time asked what your job meant to you, how would you answer him? A person in each of these Three Chairs has a different perspective on his job.

The person in the First Chair sees his job as his "vocation." The word "vocation" actually comes from the root word "to call." Who "called" whom? Why did the person who did the calling do so in the first place? Upon receiving this calling, what was the called person supposed to do? The First Chair person holds firmly to the belief that what he does for a living is a result of the Lord's call upon his life. The nature of the work isn't necessarily the issue; what is the issue is that he believes the Lord has called him to do a particular work. Remember, the First Chair person not only *knows the Lord* and *knows the works*, but also *serves the Lord*. So he works for the Lord at his job as well.

If an individual believes that he is working for the Lord, he had better have a settled confidence that he is doing exactly what the Lord wants him to do. And, as you'll discover in later chapters, the First Chair Christian is willing to do whatever the Lord makes clear is His will. In my work with the evangelistic organization called The CoMission, lay men and women all over America are uprooting from their previous "calling" because they have been newly called to move to the former Soviet Union and serve the Lord. First Chair people view their work as a calling from God, and they do their job to please Him.

Second Chair people view their work from a completely different perspective. To begin with, they have a tendency to divide people into two categories: religious people and "normal" people. They have decided that the Lord probably does "call" religious people to go onto the mission field, but He doesn't "call" normal people. Work for most folks is simply the use of their abilities to make a living. So, when the Second Chair person makes a decision about his vocation, it is usually based on what job pays the best, or which position offers the best situation geographically or culturally. Money and the type of people or organization with whom a Second Chair person feels most comfortable are the two primary factors in selecting a career. He is not all that concerned about the "call of God."

Second Chair people don't wake up in the morning with the question, "Well, Lord, I dedicate this day to You. What in particular would You like me to do for You?" That's outside their frame of reference. I've traveled across the world challenging Christians in many different cultures and contexts. The vast majority have never asked this question, mainly because they are not sold out to the Lord. They remain committed to their own interests and decisions. Their ears are shut to God's calling because their hearts haven't opened to His leading. They have so many conditions and excuses and "buts" that the din in their mind is deafening to the small, quiet voice of the Master. The fabric on the middle chair is woven with the preferences of the person who sits in it, not by the Lord who sits on the throne above. Rather than viewing their work as a calling, they view it as an avenue to a better life.

The Third Chair person doesn't even think that such things as callings are possible. After all, they do not know God, nor, as Paul put it, are they able to discern the things of the Spirit. No matter how they may try, or how smart they may be, or how much wisdom they may have acquired, they cannot receive the things of the Spirit. So they take jobs without any thought of calling at all. Note that this type of thinking marks the person who lives as though there is no God. For a believer to follow this pattern is more than immature; it's ungodly.

A second observation about the concept of "work" as it relates to each of the Three Chairs has to do with the perceived *result of work*. The person in the Second Chair believes that his work is the supplier of the resources from which to purchase necessary items in life. The better the job, the more resources. Thus, he believes that it is his effort which produces results.

The thought of a person in the First Chair is exactly backwards. He believes that *God* is the supplier of resources. He doesn't accept what he used to believe about work and money and provision and resources. His mind has undergone a dramatic transformation. He relies on God to provide for him. His work is to obey God's calling, even if that means doing things that don't make sense. I've known some incredibly gifted men and women who could have been making much more money working in the marketplace; instead, they chose to assist Christian ministries because they believed it was God's calling for their lives. Even though it meant less money and less prestige, they followed the Lord. In this person's mind, our jobs don't provide for our needs — God does. And our efforts don't produce the results — God does.

For those who sit in the Second Chair, that kind of thinking seems far-fetched; perhaps only a word game. But when the change comes and they are liberated to sit in the First Chair, they begin to serve the Lord. They consciously embrace the revolutionary words of Jesus Christ in the Sermon on the Mount. These words have shocked all Second and Third Chair people for nearly two millennia:

> "Therefore do not worry, saying, 'What shall we eat?' or 'What shall we drink?' or 'What shall we wear?' For after all these things the Gentiles seek (those were the Third Chair people of Jesus' day). For your *heavenly Father knows that you need all these things*. But seek first the kingdom of God and His righteousness, and *all these things shall be added to you*" (Matthew 6:31-33).

A profound difference, isn't it? Jesus told His followers to seek the exact opposite of what the Second and Third Chair people seek. Don't seek what your job will enable you to buy; rather, seek His Kingdom and His Righteousness. Don't worry about obtaining material things; God will supply all your needs. The things of this world will not last. Instead, focus on the spiritual things, which are eternal. Do you know what happens with the things that you really need? The answer is profound. Jesus said that "all" those things shall be added to you. That is written in the passive tense, so in other words, all those things will be literally *given* to you. God will take care of those who trust Him.

Jesus had a radical perspective. In its most basic form, His teaching for the First Chair is this: *"You work for My Father, and He will take care of all your needs."*

"Come on," the average Second Chair person says. "You must be kidding. How is that going to happen?"

Jesus knew we would all ask that most logical question, so He gave ample proof for any Second Chair person. In Matthew Chapter 6, He pointed out the birds to the people and said, "God takes care of them. Won't He also take care of you?" Then He pointed the flowers out and said, "God clothes the flowers in beauty. Won't He also clothe you?" God cares for us. The First Chair person knows that fact and lives accordingly. It doesn't make any sense to a person operating in this world. A person looking from the perspective of the world thinks the First Chair believer is crazy, or quaint, or perhaps just plain wrong. But being in the First Chair causes us to focus on God, not ourselves.

Don't miss the main point of this section. The First Chair person seeks God's Kingdom first, not his position in the company. He has decided he is not going to serve himself any longer. He has decided to follow Jesus, and there's no turning back. Once you've tasted the table the Lord sets for those who seek Him, nothing else seems to taste the same. Even when it's served on the best china and by the best service this world can offer, it's just not as good as the Lord's.

Does the First Chair person quit his job then? Of course not. But he has learned a very important lesson, much like King David learned nearly 3,000 years ago: though we have a job, our boss there isn't really the supplier of our resources. Ultimately, God is our boss, and the person in the First Chair knows that. The person in the Second Chair smirks at that thought. This is truth, put into practice. *God is my boss.* The difference is not marginal, it is seminal. Listen to a few of the key beliefs from the life of that famous First Chair person, King David, in 1 Chronicles 29:

> "Both riches and honor come from You...."
>
> "But who am I, and who are my people, that we should be able to offer so willingly as this? For all things come from You."

The Second Chair person works for money, prestige, power, and possessions. The First Chair person works to serve the Lord. What did you say your "profession" is? Look closely at the word "profession" because it is filled with insight. The original word has been lost to this generation. "Profession" literally means "to speak forth."

Unfortunately, the Second Chair person has separated his job from his profession rather than having his job *be* his profession. Men and women used to view who they were as one complete unit that was not divided into sections. People lived in small towns and grew up together, generation after generation. They would know me as "Jim's boy" or "old Tom's grandson." I would go to the same school as everyone else in the neighborhood, attend one of the two country churches, and buy the groceries from the corner country store, licorice jar and all. When I finished high school, I would probably follow in my father's footsteps. He would pass on his skills to his son as his father had before him. I'd marry one of the village families' daughters, and probably join the young married softball team. The heritage was rich and heavily woven together. That's the way things often worked in this country. That is, until the last two generations.

Now, you can live in a neighborhood for a decade and not know the name of your neighbor who lives two doors down. You can work in a company where not one of your neighbors or any family member work. You can attend your favorite church, 27 miles away from your home, where no one knows you. And you can join the YMCA softball team where there's a completely different group of people to get to know. Our lives are splintered. They lack cohesion and a unifying theme. That's what our culture is like. So now, you are free to be one person at work and another at home, a third at church and still another at the ball game or at the club. Since no one knows you in any other context, you can "reinvent" yourself for each one. Instead of a social fabric that insures that we are the same in each setting, we have a social fabric that does the exact opposite—it tempts us to play situation ethics to satisfy us at that particular moment in time, and it allows us to do so. We have divided ourselves from one into many.

Soon, however, the "many" aren't one anymore. Your ethics in business or sportsmanship on the field may be very different from what you are in your church suit and tie. We have a phrase for that today: a lack of integrity. "Integrity" actually means "oneness," so a person trying to play many parts that don't fit easily together lacks that oneness. He or she has no integrity.

Not only do we have a lack of integrity in our society but we have fully embraced that a lack of integrity is entirely the way to go! That's why we can vote for a president who may be skilled in the role of politics but who has completely opposite lifestyle, values, and convictions than we have. We have decided that success in one role can have absolutely nothing to do with how the person is in other roles. The same has become true in church circles. Pastors can divorce time and time again, yet still be kept on as the pastor because they preach so well. Apparently those congregations reason that his speaking ability has nothing to do with his personal life. But God has made clear that we cannot separate the two. Who you are when no one's looking is just as important to God as who you are when you are standing in plain view—whether you are a pastor or not. God does not see anything the same way people do. People look at the outside of a person, but the Lord looks at the heart. He seeks integrity in the lives of His people.

In this culture, we tend to see our lives as a chest of drawers, compartmentalized. One drawer is for this part of my life and another drawer is for another part. Eventually, our lives are made of many completely separate elements. In each drawer are the different clothes we wear, the different words we speak, and the different values that we choose to carry. The biblical word for a person who lives life like a chest of drawers is "hypocrite."

As you may know, the word "hypocrite" originally came from the stage, where the same actor or actress would perform as different people by changing the mask that covered his or her face. The slang word for this is "two-faced." Unfortunately, that describes many Christians today.

Now, this may appear on the surface to be quite distant from how the Three Chairs think about their jobs, but it really isn't. It is right at the heart of the matter. Your concept of what a "profession" is helps define who you are. The Second Chair person uses drawers to separate his life. For every new situation he encounters, another drawer is added to insure complete appropriateness. When he is at church, he pulls out the "spiritual" drawer. When he plays basketball with the guys, he pulls out the "athlete" drawer. Rather than having a oneness, an integrity to his character, he *plays* characters.

But when the First Chair person left the Second Chair, the only thing he brought with him was the top drawer, where all the crucial and real things are kept. Being "one" is all-important to the First Chair person because he knows that *integrity* is the characteristic that is most highly treasured by the courts of heaven.

The Second Chair person seeks the treasures of the halls of business, and we all know that business and religion don't mix in this society. Nobody wants God to step into the elevator with him. And leave that Bible at home, where it belongs. When you are out on a business lunch, don't get hung up on praying–do that later, on your own time. That's the mentality of the Second Chair. He has to separate his spiritual life from his business life. In doing so, he loses his integrity.

I once attended a large Christian conference with a friend. We were on the way to visit the booths during the break when my partner spotted someone nearly four aisles away. He shouted his name in surprise, and I followed him as he went to meet that other person. The two men looked at each other, kind of shocked and embarrassed. Finally, one of them said, "I didn't expect to see *you* here!" and the other one said, "Well, I didn't expect to see *you* here either!" Then, there was another awkward pause.

"You aren't a Christian, are you?" the other person asked.

"Well....yes, I am," my friend said. "Are you?"

"Yes, for thirty years!"

They then embraced each other like long lost family members, laughed too loudly, and went their ways.

My friend said something I'll long remember: "I can't believe that. We've worked in the next office from each other for twenty years. I never knew he was a Christian until today."

How could that be? Only one way–Second Chair Christianity!

Both men had decided that it was wisest to keep their faith in Christ undercover in the business world. They lived out of other drawers at work for twenty years. They both felt some embarrassment and carefully veiled shame at their discovery. Somewhere in their hearts, they knew something was wrong with what had just happened, but they were unable to put their fingers on it.

Let me put my finger right on it for a moment. That interchange proved that neither man were First Chair believers. Why? Because First Chair believers are believers *first* and business persons second. They serve the Lord *first*. First Chair believers would have leaked their values, convictions, testimony, prayer, and lifestyle all over their workplace. In fact, they have the respect of the office because they take a stand with wisdom and conviction.

You see, First Chair believers see their jobs the way previous generations did–as a profession. The First Chair believer seeks the kingdom of God and His righteousness first, discovers God's calling through which to best serve Him, and then builds a strong platform of integrity upon which to profess the truth about Jesus Christ to all who would have ears to hear. They seek not just to live what they believe, but to "profess" it openly and naturally. Within those daily choices of integrity, honesty, faithfulness, loyalty, steadfastness, competence, and reliability, the First Chair person carefully builds that platform upon which to "speak forth," to profess what lies in the heart—from life to lips, so to speak. They earn the right to speak the truth about God to the people with whom they rub shoulders on a daily basis. That's the pattern of the First Chair Christian. The Second Chair person separates his faith from the marketplace. You only have to see a few actions and attitudes to discern the Chairs in which most of the people you meet are sitting. Where are you, my friend?

THE ROLE OF FAMILY IN THE THREE CHAIRS

The Bible has many different words to describe First, Second, and Third Chair people. In fact, as you become more and more acquainted with its overall themes, you may find the Three Chairs on almost every page of the Bible.

One word used in the New Testament to describe a First Chair person is "elder," as Paul used in his writings, referring to a leader in a church. In 1 Timothy 3:1-7, Paul lists key integrity issues. An elder must be blameless, the husband of one wife, temperate, sober-minded, of good behavior, hospitable, able to teach, not given to wine, not violent, not greedy, gentle, not quarrelsome, not covetous. All those words are character words. Character traits are never to be divided among the different roles we fulfill in our life. Character simply reflects who we are. What you appear to be is what you should be—the same in every location and in every place.

You may have noticed that I purposefully skipped the one characteristic of an "elder" that received more attention in I Timothy 3 than any of the others. In fact, there are more words to emphasize that characteristic than all of the above added together! Read carefully: "An elder must be...one who rules his own house well, having his own children in submission with all reverence. For if a man does not know how to rule his own house, how will he take care of the church of God?"

Consider four key points in these verses:

1. The First Chair man must rule his house in a certain way: "well."

2. The First Chair man has his children in submission to him.

3. The First Chair man sees his children submit to him in a certain way: "with all reverence."

4. The First Chair man validates that he is qualified to lead the church of God by how effectively he has led his house.

First Chair men raise their children in a certain manner. First Chair men rule their house in a certain manner. First Chair men disciple their children so that they have learned the importance of submission to authority. First Chair men earn the genuine respect of their children so that they submit to their fathers with a heartfelt attitude of reverence. In other words, the family of the First Chair man has characteristics regarding the nature of his home and the attitude and actions of his children toward him that anyone can identify.

This remarkable linkage between the life of the father and the behavior of the children is the Lord's, not man's. The Lord views the influence of a father upon his children as being a direct reflection of the character of the man! And if the father has the character qualities just listed (blameless, temperate, hospitable, *et al*), do you think it will be difficult for a child to submit?

You probably know of some families that fit this description. But for every one like that, how many others can we describe where the opposite is the truth? Being a man or woman of character is not enough to build a godly home. Character is the foundation of everything else, to be sure, but brick and mortar must also be added for the family to truly be a First Chair family. What is God's heart regarding your family? The answer might surprise you. In Malachi Chapter 2, God has a conversation with a large group of Second and Third Chair people who are complaining because He is not answering their prayers. They are obviously upset, their suffering so intense that when they pray, they "flood the altar" with their tears. And still, God will not answer! Wait until you see His shocking reason. In this passage, He reveals the difference between the First and Second Chair person's family.

The Prophet of the Lord speaking to the people:

"And this is the second thing you do:
You cover the altar of the Lord with tears,
with weeping and crying;
So He does not regard the offering anymore,
Nor receive it with good will from your hands." (v. 13)

"Yet you say,
'For what reason?'" (*In other words, Why won't the Lord answer our prayer and regard our offering?*)

"Because the Lord has been witness (*the Lord has seen what you've done*)
Between you and the wife of your youth,
with whom you have dealt treacherously (*the husbands are being unfaithful to their wives*);
yet she is your companion and your wife by covenant."
(v. 14)
(*The Lord reveals later in the chapter that they are divorcing their wives.*)

"But did He not make them one, (*God made husband and wife to be one*)
Having a remnant of the Spirit?

And why one!
(*Now this is the key issue–why did God make marriage?*)

He seeks godly offspring" (v. 15).

Did you see it? Marriage is not only for companionship and for fulfilling His creation commands; the Lord is seeking something from your marriage. Something more than you might ever expect. The Lord God is seeking offspring–children from your marriage. But, a certain kind of offspring. *God seeks from you godly offspring!*

Unlike the one time in the universe when God created two human beings in the Garden of Eden, the rest of all offspring were to come through the marriage covenant relationships of men and women. What God is seeking is not just children, but children who have been raised to choose the way of the Lord Jesus Christ. The Lord wants you to have full integrity and to walk worthy of your calling–and then bring your boys and girls right along with you. They are to be walking in your footsteps. Embracing your values. Serving your God. Choosing your Lord to be their Lord. The Lord wants you to pass the torch of godliness to the next generation!

The First Chair person raises godly children; the Second Chair person raises children. This isn't by accident, either. It's not by chance. Godly children are developed only through intense purpose, perseverance, and prayer; through temporary failures and setbacks; through the ups and downs in the seasons of life. Beneath it all, deep in the heart of the First Chair person is the resolve to fulfill God's deep dream—to offer back to Him godly offspring.

Listen to one of the First Chair believers express this purpose nearly 3,500 years ago: "But for me and my house, we will serve the Lord." Do you see that conjunctive word "and" linking "me" and "my house"? Joshua understood the purpose of the family. It is to raise children who serve the Lord. There is a link between your godly character and your determined discipleship of your children so that they grow into godly adults.

Look once again at Joshua's timeless words and sense with me his intense commitment: "We *will* serve the Lord." Did you notice what word was missing that seems to be in all of our conversation about families today? It is the word "*try*." The contemporary Christian would say, "I'm going to try to encourage my family to walk with the Lord," or "I'm going to do the best I can to see that my family walks with the Lord." Why is that word missing from the lips of Joshua? For the same reason that it isn't missing from the list of qualifications for an elder in the church of God. "Try" implies that it really doesn't work. "So as long as I do my part, then I certainly can't be held accountable for my children's actions of rebellion or attitude of irreverence." But if we aren't accountable, then how can the Lord list it as a requirement for the elder's behavior? And how can Joshua say with such boldness, "But for me and my house, we *will* serve the Lord"?

Mind you, Joshua didn't say those words in a corner, hidden away from the ears and eyes of anyone who might be watching. Rather, he is giving a public speech in front of every member of the nation of Israel—including those who knew him and his family best.

Does that mean that the First Chair person never stumbles? Never sins greatly? Unfortunately not. David committed adultery. Abraham tried to pass his wife off as his sister because he was afraid others would kill him if they wanted his beautiful wife. Don't misunderstand the reality of the individual's free choice in the matter—as children grow up and start making their own decisions, those decisions are their own. But neither should we dismiss the profound reality of God's seeking heart expressed by His requirements for the elder, nor the bold statement of Joshua. Second Chair people invest their time and energy in providing for their children, keeping them busy and involved, and driving them to multiple religious activities. Second Chair people hope things will work out. Second Chair people pass off the responsibility to others, rather than building into the heart and soul of their children the integrity, character, commitment, sacrifice, and purpose needed to be a person of the First Chair.

The Lord confronts Second Chair people with directness and accountability. In one of the most tragic and heart-wrenching stories in the entire Bible, the High Priest of Israel, Eli, raised two sons who served as priests under his house and his authority. Unfortunately, they rebelled against Eli and the Lord in blatant ways. Their story is described in 1 Samuel Chapter 2.

"Now the sons of Eli were corrupt, they did not know the Lord. (*They weren't saved.*)

Therefore the sin of the young men (*his two boys*) was very great before the Lord, for men abhorred the offering of the Lord." (*They treated worship with disrespect.*)

"Now Eli was very old; and he heard everything his sons did to all Israel, and how they lay with the women who assembled at the door of the tabernacle of meeting." (*They were involved in sexual sin, even though they were supposed to be the spiritual leaders of Israel.*)

"So he said to them, 'Why do you do such things? For I hear of your evil dealings from all the people. No, my sons! For it is not a good report that I hear. You make the Lord's people transgress.'" (*Their sin caused others to sin also.*)

Now observe carefully what the Lord's evaluation of Eli is at this point. Eli had verbally rebuked his sons, which may be the basis for dismissing his responsibility for what his sons were doing. But the point that must be made is that the Lord evaluated Eli even though his two sons were grown by this point. Here's what the Lord Himself says directly to Eli and not to his sons:

"Why do you (Eli) kick at My sacrifice and My offering which I have commanded in My habitation, and honor your sons more than Me, to make yourselves fat with the best of all the offerings of Israel My people?" (1 Samuel 2:29).

"Far be it from Me, for those who honor Me I will honor, and those who despise Me shall be lightly esteemed" (v. 30b).

Even as I type this, my heart breaks once again over this tragic story of another Christian leader who lived generations before me. The end of the story only gets worse as it reveals the Lord's holy judgment on a father and his sons. The sons were put to death in a battle with the Philistines, and Eli, upon hearing the news, fell backward off his chair and broke his neck. The Ark of the Covenant was captured by an enemy, and Israel was in such despair that the High Priest's grandchild was named *Ichabod*, which means "the glory has departed." The glory of God had indeed departed from the land.

The main point to be taken from this record is that the Lord's description of Eli proves he was indeed a Second Chair believer. He was not serving the Lord first, and the Lord was not number one in his life; his boys were. In fact, in the Lord's eyes, Eli "despised" God. Eli didn't raise his children to honor the Lord because he had succumbed to using the ministry for personal pleasure rather than to honor the Lord. Instead of following the Bible's clear revelation regarding the meat offered by the people of Israel, he allowed his sons to defraud the Lord and to personally take "the best of all the offerings of Israel My people...to make yourself fat."

That's always at the root. If you dig deep enough, you will always uncover the real reasons why the children are not raised as godly offspring. The parent has another god before the Lord. The parent is seeking something that the Lord does not approve, rather than seeking to raise children that are indeed godly.

In America, that god seems most frequently to be the love of money, the "good life." Fathers work all the time, saying that they are doing it for their children. But they're not; they are doing it for themselves. One thing is certain: they are not doing it for the Lord! Sin multiplies upon sin, and soon wives are moving into the marketplace, turning their children over to the childcare center down the street. Many times, the mother is working simply to help pay the bills acquired by buying a bigger house or a larger car or a finer vacation. These are the things that are more highly valued by a Second Chair parent, rather than investing deeply in the lives of those children. Second Chair Christian parents give away the very heart of what God has entrusted to them: raising godly offspring. Instead, they simply raise offspring. In Samuel's day, they would have said it like this: "You entrust your children to be raised by the Canaanites so you can raise a large crop in your fields."

Heaven is not shouting with affirmation about what is happening in too many churches today. If you think it is, your TV is turned up too loud. The divorce rate in the churches of our country—not only among non-Christians—is more than 50 percent of all who get married. The trauma to the children of divorce is finally being admitted as the rape it is in their lives. Only one step removed from the physical divorce of mothers and fathers is an emotional divorce. No wonder God was so furious with the people for divorcing. He created the family for the very purpose of fulfilling His dream of godly offspring, and the likelihood of that in the face of divorce is very small.

The average Christian man spends less than 2 minutes a day per child. The average Christian woman with children who works full-time outside of the home cannot spend much more. Raising godly offspring is the most challenging and all-encompassing assignment God has ever given to us. In fact, the family is the greenhouse where the Lord grooms and prepares the leaders of His glorious church. You must first learn character, competence, and conviction in your home; then you can be ready to lead in His Home–the Church of Christ.

Second Chair people find reasons they cannot disciple their kids. Second Chair people try, but First Chair people do it. First Chair people have no other gods or goals before the Lord. That's why you can watch their children and see their faith growing, you can sense their heart as they make hard and distressful but necessary choices. That's why heaven shouts with joy when another family chooses the way of heaven while on earth–they dedicate themselves to fulfilling God's dream.

Yes, Joshua, yes! "But for me and my house, we *will* serve the Lord."

1. How is your work a calling?

2. Does the illustration of the "drawers" describe you? Are you a different person in one setting than you are in another? Why?

3. Describe the difference in perspective on work between a First Chair believer and a Second Chair believer.

4. According to Malachi 2, what does God desire from our marriages?

5. How can we best develop that?

CHAPTER THREE

The Role of the Church in The Three Chairs

The principle of the Three Chairs applies not only to people and families, but to churches, denominations, Christian colleges and seminaries, mission organizations, parachurch ministries, and even Christian-owned companies. The principles apply for two reasons. First, the purpose of all these particular organizations is to accomplish biblical goals and objectives. Second, these organizations are usually composed of believers sitting in one of the first two Chairs. As a result, each organization will reflect the characteristics of whichever Chair its members are sitting in. Their corporate behavior is predictable. Their values reflect the same values as an individual life reflects, since an organization is merely the enlargement of a group into one entity.

THE CHURCH IN THE WORLD

You will know which Chair a church sits in simply by looking at the behaviors of those who attend. Third Chair churches have lost the Bible in the rubble as Christianity collapsed. Usually, their pastors are more liberal than the congregation and have been schooled in the heresies of a bankrupt faith. To them, the Bible is nothing more than another book from which to select stories applicable to the homily of the day. They don't know the Lord and, since they've neglected their Bibles, they don't even know His work. Third Chair churches are dead — like the church of Sardis in Revelation Chapter 3. They were warned to wake up, for they had the truth but would not repent and obey it. And now, their names have been blotted out of the Book of Life.

Second Chair churches have their Bibles, and the people usually bring them to church. As you learned in the first chapter, they "know the Lord" and "know the works which He has done." They honor the Word, and can usually find the passage being read during the sermon because the majority have been raised at the feet of committed parents. The Bible is viewed as the backbone of the sermon and is usually read at the beginning, then used as the "springboard" for the pastor to launch into his own thoughts, stories, illustrations, and encouragement. Like the church at Laodicea, also in Revelation Chapter 3, Second Chair churches have deeds, activity, and orthodoxy. But there isn't any fire to it. They're lukewarm toward God. They believe that they are rich and in need of nothing, but, just as the Lord said to the believers at Laodicea, "You do not realize that you are wretched, pitiful, poor, blind, and naked." They have the truth, but they assume that simply having the truth is enough. Rather than a vibrant relationship with Christ, they've got a ho-hum acquaintance with Him. The Bible is rarely opened between Sundays, and they don't give any authority to its principles to impact their lives.

First Chair churches honor the Bible. More than that, the people are hungry for it. By the time they enter the sanctuary, the people are full of anticipation for a word from the Scriptures. Unlike the Second Chair church, the pastor of a First Chair church aims the Word of God right at the heart of the congregation. He preaches with good, old-fashioned "unction," and the congregation experiences the conviction of the Holy Spirit frequently. Repentance is common among its members. Deep soul-searching often results when the Sword of the Spirit is unleashed. The Bible is seen as the authority of life–it is fully embraced as the final and full answer to the heart-wrenching problems of marriage, family, personal character, values, parenting, business success, and societal dilemmas. The pastor who is in the First Chair doesn't value his own ideas; rather, he views himself as a servant of the Word of God. He is only the mouthpiece for the Spirit of God, the "John the Baptist," moving among the flock with tenderness and power. First Chair believers are able to reflect the Bible in their daily walk.

Third Chair churches see the Bible as a relic of bygone days. Second Chair churches see the Bible as a helpful guide. First Chair churches see the Bible as living, vital revelation from God, given directly to them for whatever their needs are that very day. Third Chair church families have large family Bibles in cases. Second Chair church families carry their Bibles to church but use it rarely between Sundays. First Chair families feast upon the Bible and use it regularly.

Let me approach this all important issue of the Bible's prominence in the life of the church from one more perspective—how the individual members determine what is right and what is wrong in the ebb and flow of daily life. The First Chair person has come to a deep conviction regarding who is in charge of his life—he chooses God. Therefore, he soon comes to the firm conclusion that God's Word must be the authority for his life. He submits to the authority of the Bible and seeks to understand it in order to live it. First Chair people look at the Bible as the source of what to do, not just what to know. Their lives are filled with complexities and challenges, but because they have lost the root of pride and arrogance that people in the Second Chair have, they know that only God's wisdom offers the true and life-giving answers. Therefore, they have chosen to submit to the Bible. It's commandments are their choices. The Scriptures are supreme.

The Second Chair person believes that the Bible is God's Word, but he has kind of stalled on the submission issue. He believes in the Bible, but his beliefs haven't reached the level of conviction. Simple belief is not strong enough to stand up against the consistent pressures of life, but conviction rules a person even in the most difficult times. The Second Chair person has a different source of authority in his life, so he is not well-grounded or strengthened by convictions. The person who has the Bible as his authority in life is able to stand firm in the face of any persecution while the individual who can't rely on his Bible will wilt in the face of the slightest persecution. And I have found this to be universally true in every context I have been in.

For the Second Chair Christian, the factor that determines what values should be embraced is not the commands of Scripture but the customary practices of his fellow Christians. This difference isn't even recognized by the vast majority of Second Chair believers because the difference is subtle—subtle but deadly. Rather than allowing the infallible God to lead them, they allow fallible humans to tell them what to do. The commands of Scripture are fully inspired by God and therefore reliable in every context of life; other Christians are not inspired by God and are many times not only unreliable but completely contradictory to the Bible. The First Chair believer chooses the Bible over other believers. The Second Chair Christian chooses other Christians over the commandments. And here is one powerful difference: the commands of Scripture haven't changed in thousands of years because they are absolute truth. But Christians who are not anchored in absolute truth have been constantly changing all along. Even First Chair Christians through the ages have had some major differences of opinion!

It's because of this very thing that the First Chair church preaches the Bible very differently from the Second Chair church. In one, the people desperately need the Truth because they do not trust their own devices; in the other, people trust themselves and are "fine" without a real meal from the table of the Lord. In one context, a person will leave starving if the Word is not preached; in the other, a person will leave bored. The difference is remarkable.

Picture the Three Chairs again, but instead of people sitting on them, picture churches. Underneath the First Chair lies the Bible — an anchor against the storms of life. Under the Third Chair lies the world, with its sensual pleasures, materialism, and pride. The church in the Third Chair has turned away from the Bible, and is solidly entrenched in the things of the world. Only traces of true

Christianity can be found. These two churches are at opposite ends of the spiritual scale. And the Second Chair church sits in the middle, trying to decide which way to go.

As the world spins in direct opposition to the Bible and the ways of God, you'll notice that the Third Chair church is attached to the world and spins with it. From the pulpits of the Third Chair churches are preached such blasphemes as that Jesus is not the Son of God, that God is love without any degree of holiness and judgment, that man is good and not sinful, and that salvation is merely becoming all that you can be. Forever it turns, like a top out of control, on a purposeful arc away from the Bible and its "old-fashioned" beliefs. As the Bible unmistakably teaches, the world has nothing to do with the Lord, and it is an enemy of God and the cross of · Christ.

Now let's consider the church in the middle. On one side is the Bible and on the other side is the world. But here's a surprise for them: a person or a church in the Second Chair cannot remain in the middle indefinitely. In time, he or it will be drawn closer to one pole or the other. You see, the middle ground is one of compromise—a futile attempt to mix the kingdom of Satan with the kingdom of God. The problem is, no matter how hard you try, the two will not become one. The two cannot become one. The Second Chair church must be drawn toward one or the other.

Whether or not a person believes it, the Bible makes it clear that there are only two kingdoms, not three. There is the Kingdom of God and the Kingdom of Satan. We do not have the Kingdom of God, the Kingdom of Satan, and the Kingdom of Man. Man worships and serves either one or the other. Man's belief that he rules his own kingdom is only a figment of his arrogance and pride.

For the vast majority of Second Chair churches, the magnet of the world is more enticing than the invitation of the Lord. So, the middle church typically tilts its steeple toward the sky scrapers of industry and commerce, of wanton pleasure and reckless abandon. The Second Chair church is populated with people who know the Lord, carry His Word, sing hymns to Him, and take a stand for the major doctrines of the Bible. Unfortunately, they have not moved their heart membership to the First Chair, to join the Church of the committed. Instead, their membership remains comfortably in the Church of the compromisers. Seeking the comfortable luke-warm waters of neither the hot nor the cold, rather, desiring some of each, they seek to keep the two in a tolerable union. Here it is that, thousands of years later, the deceit of the enemy still entices mankind to pluck the forbidden fruit from his seemingly endless orchard.

The Second Chair church slowly, nearly imperceptibly, inches toward the world and toward being what Revelation calls the Harlot Church. The call of Christ and the pull of the world are both working against the middle, both seeking victory accomplished only by the movement from the middle. When that church moves en mass toward the First Chair, we describe it as "revival." That which was once alive but became dead over time has now been revived. When that middle church moves toward the world, we describe it as a church that died or "became liberal." The life that used to flow in its sanctuary fled into the night. *Ichabod* is etched in the mantle above the baptismal pool. The glory of the Lord departs.

It's only through hindsight that a person can see what happened. Only by comparing where a church was five years ago to where it is today can we know which direction a church is moving, whether toward God or toward Satan. When a Second Chair church follows the spin of the world, it usually trails by about ten years. The compromising church is never up-to-date in the depth of sin and abandonment of the world. It's not hard to see that the values and practices the world had a decade ago have become the values and the practices of many churches today.

You can see the scrape marks on the floor under the Second Chair church—inch after inch, it has moved away from the Lord. No single inch seems very big, but if you look back over twenty years, you can see that those inches soon become feet, then yards, then....

But stop for a moment. Look in the opposite direction. Look back toward the committed church, those in the First Chair. To your shock and confusion, it is very far away, almost on the other side of the world—so far removed, so far out of touch, so out of step with the times. How could that be? Only for one reason: when it comes to the essentials of commitment to Jesus Christ, the church in the First Chair has not moved during the last twenty years. In fact, it has not moved during the last 2,000 years. It has remained true to the absolute standards of the Bible, a bulwark never failing.

Go back twenty years to the 1970's. What are a couple of the things that made scratches on the floor as the Second Chair church followed the leadership of the world? There was probably a time when you saw the first movie that made you extremely uncomfortable. Perhaps you blushed in shame. Perhaps you got up and left the theater. You couldn't believe it! How could they put that trash out? Why would anyone go see it?

Now fast forward to the last thirty days of your personal life and the lives of your friends at church. What movies have you seen? In the past month, many of your church friends, and maybe even you, have watched R-rated movies with explicit sex, nudity, scores of swear words, multiple adulterous relationships, and many other things. It seems that entertainment consists of scenes depicting immorality, especially of young teens, and graphic violence of the most riveting nature. Listen to the conversation after Sunday school between church friends who are discussing the latest R-rated thriller breaking records at the box office: "You've just got to go and see this one—it's unbelievable. There're a few spots which aren't very good, but besides that, it's a must-see."

Now, stop for a minute. Do you think I'm exaggerating? Let me give you three first-hand experiences so that you can see life through my eyes for a moment.

The first one occurred when Walk Thru the Bible was in the midst of launching the YouthWalk Magazine a few years ago. Our staff did a lot of research before we wrote even one word or selected one photo, just to be sure we knew where the young people were coming from. One of the experiments I undertook back then was to find out what teens were watching. I visited the local video store and interviewed the management about the ten hottest videos on the market. Almost all of them were R-rated. I then put all of them on a list, but I didn't include the ratings. We made hundreds of copies and had them distributed around Atlanta to all kinds of both religious and secular groups of teens. It was a simple test–all we put on the top of the page was the following: "This is a market research project for the launch of a new national youth magazine. Please check the movies/videos you have seen thus far."

We obviously didn't put "Walk Thru the Bible" on the top, as that would skew the data. We passed the flyer out to thousands of teens, then we compiled the results. I'll never forget the afternoon when we put the results across the whiteboard in our headquarters' Creative Center. It was stunning. There was almost no difference between the lists. The youths at the most biblical churches in Atlanta saw the same videos as young people who didn't know the Lord. Christian young people had seen, on average, only one fewer R-rated movie than non-Christians. As I drove home that night I was in shock. I can remember, in the middle of Atlanta traffic, mulling over the question, "Where did they see those movies?" The answer came like a punch to my heart–in the living rooms of their homes. If we're going to compromise our moral integrity by watching filthy entertainment at home, we can expect that our kids will pick up the same habit—probably at a very young age. When we take any step that compromises, we influence our families.

A second eye-opener came when our oldest daughter called from her girlfriend's home while she was on a sleep-over with a few other church friends. She was having a great time, but she had a question. They were about to watch a movie. She knew our family standards, so she called to see what we would say. She told me the name of the movie–it was rated PG-13. Our daughter was in her pre-teens, and we said "no." But then we got to thinking about the situation. Why were Christian parents allowing their young daughter to watch PG-13 movies? What did that say about the moral standards of *their* personal lives?

I have one other example, one I have yet to come to grips with. It's not about my daughter's peers; it's about my own. It's not about the youth of today; it's about the Christian leaders, pastors, and parachurch leaders whom I run with. More than 2,000 of us convened for a very large and influential annual meeting, taking over most of a huge hotel for a few days. We met from morning to night. One of my friends was an acquaintance of the Executive Manager of this huge complex, and he had been witnessing to him for years. My friend was sharing what a remarkable difference the Lord made in his life and family—how God had changed his values and lifestyle. The Executive Manager sensed that this may be something he was looking for. Until check-out time.

My friend was standing next to the revolving doors waiting for a taxi to the airport when the Executive Manager came up to say good-bye. He seemed a bit flustered, perhaps even depressed. As the taxi approached the revolving door, he asked one question of my friend: "I just got the records from last night. You know, your convention nearly filled up every room we had. All these religious leaders. But I'm confused. Can you explain to me why more than 50 percent of the rooms last night watched X-rated videos?"

As the world turns, so spins a Second Chair church. The people in it are willing to compromise so they can get along with the world. This is true not only in their movie habits but in their marriages as well. Take another trip in your time machine to the 1970's. Name the couples in your church who got divorced during that decade. You probably won't even be able to fill one hand, no matter how large your church and circle of Christian friends may be.

Now, back to the present, start counting your Christian friends and family members that are divorced in the 1990's. If you are like Darlene and me, you'll be able to count literally dozens and dozens. Half of you reading this page have experienced a divorce or are even considering one right at this moment. What is the point of this litany? Only this: the church in the Second Chair follows ten paces behind, in the steps of the world. In the past three years, I would say it has moved closer to five or six steps behind. What the world does, the compromisers copy. That's one of the patterns woven into the cushion of the Second Chair.

What about the First Chair church? To be certain, no church is without its problems. But within the ranks of the truly committed, you'll see a vast difference in a whole range of personal and family values. Often, however, those believers will feel isolated. They're a bit "odd" or "old-fashioned," and they almost over-embrace you when they find another family who shares the *same* values. But why should they be surprised? We didn't invent these values! They are very clearly right there in the Bible–and they are just as definitive about what is right and what is wrong today as they were in the 1970's or in the 1950's or the year 100 AD. The Truth is still the Truth. The First Chair church is unabashedly resolute on its commitment to the Word of God as the sole standard of life and behavior, while the Second Chair quotes from the pulpit interesting lines from R-rated movies just to make his point.

Let's summarize:

First Church	Middle Church	World Church
Lives by what the *commandments* of the Bible teach	Lives by what their fellow *Christians* do and believe is right to do	Lives by what the people in their *Culture* do at work and circle of friends
Scripture is the basis	*Saints* are the basis	*Society* is the basis
"What does God want?"	"What do you think?"	"Who cares what you do?"
The *Bible* standards of behavior are *absolutes* regardless of the culture	The *Believers* standards of behavior are following the footsteps of the culture	The *Basic* standards of behavior are what is right in your own eyes
What's right in God's eyes	What's right in your eyes	What's right in my eyes

The principle of the Three Chairs is relevant to your work, your family, and your church. The difference between people sitting in each of the Three Chairs is not one of *degree* of difference; it is in the *nature* of the difference. People in the First Chair are not twenty-five percent or fifty percent better than those in the other Chairs; rather, they are completely different—with revolutionary and radical differences.

No matter how someone in the Second Chair may strain and struggle to become something different, they will always just become simply a "better" or "worse" Second-Chair sitter. Moving from one Chair to the other is nothing less than a revolutionary, total-life transformation. Though you are still, in one sense, the same person, God has made sure you are no longer the person you used to be. It's not the *amount* of change, but the *nature* of change. You aren't *better* than you used to be; that would be a serious understatement! Rather, you are *different* from what you used to be.

This book is written for the intended you—the "you" that the Lord beckons to come out from the soul of the current you. It is written for the new man that Christ suffered, died, and rose again to set free in your heart. This new person is the promise of Christ in you, the hope of glory. My purpose in writing this book is simple and straightforward: my goal is to tear away the blinders from your eyes and permit you to see the heart of the Lord. My goal is to help you learn to let God rip away the hard, callused spots surrounding your heart so He can liberate you to experience the reality of walking with the Lord.

This book came from my own transformation, so I know that it's possible for you. Transformation didn't come easy, nor did it come quickly. Instead, it has been birthed out of the depths of suffering and the fiery heat of God's purifying torch. Transformation comes out of intense seasons in the Scripture and long periods of communion with Christ. It comes as a gift from the Great Giver of All Gifts. It is only by His grace and His transforming power that anyone can ever hope or dream of becoming a true, First Chair believer. My wife and I can both speak clearly about the comfort of the Second Chair because that's where we both lived for decades. This book isn't a knowledge book, really—at the heart, it is an open chapter testifying to the grace of God past, present and future in our lives. The lessons that He has taught us and is still teaching us have been part of the process of transforming us into the very image of His Son.

You may be at a point in your pilgrimage where you find yourself aching for more of the True God than you seem to be able to find. Your ache has called forth a searching, seeking heart that beats strongly for the Lord. You have tasted, and you want more, more of Him. You have quenched your parched lips at His fountain of living waters, and you want to follow the stream to its source. You want Christ, and you'll settle for nothing different, nothing less, and nothing else.

That's good, my friend. I know those longings of the heart, and I have traveled along the banks of that stream. I have cried out in the darkness to find the Pearl of Great Price—and would have given everything I owned just to find Him.

But the Second Chair bound me to mediocrity and defeat. No matter how hard I tried, I could not get into the First Chair while sitting in the Second Chair. I would strain. And struggle. And sigh. And wonder if the life that Jesus talked so unabashedly about really existed. And if it did, could I ever find it?

When Jesus told the man who had been blind to open his eyes, the man didn't see anything new—he saw what had been there all along; he just had not been able to perceive it. When Jesus opened the man's eyes, everything changed for that man. When Christ told the man who had been crippled all his life to stand and leave the mat that had held him for decades, the man got to his feet and never again returned to the old ways.

When you discover the secrets behind opening your eyes and leaving your mat, you will never again look back over your shoulder and wish for the good old days. Those days were the old days, but in comparison to life in the First Chair, they surely were not the good days. When you rise from your Second or perhaps Third Chair to take the hand of the Master, He Himself seats you in that First Chair as an honored member of His family of overcomers. You will never leave your seat at His table. You won't look back. In fact, you'll only have one thought that flicks across your consciousness:

"Why did it take me so long to move to the First Chair?"

The goal of this book is to help you release your grip on the soft Second Chair, to encourage you to believe—really believe—that what Jesus said is truly the answer you have been looking for. You see, the First Chair is the Chair of the abundant, overflowing life. And this is the Chair Jesus has reserved for you. Come, my friend, sit in front of the fire.

Come now.

1. What is Christ's message to the church at Sardis in Revelation 3:1-6?

2. How was the church at Laodicea a Second Chair church (see Revelation 3:14-22)?

3. In your own words, what is Christ's response to those Second Chair believers?

4. What are some of the ways you have seen the church compromise with the world in recent years?

5. In Revelation 2:1-7, what prescription does the Lord offer the church at Ephesus, a group of Christians who had allowed their strong faith to turn into a cold orthodoxy? How can we put that into practice?

Developing First Hand Faith

CHAPTER FOUR

Commitment, Compromise, and Conflict

If you are to get well, you have to first be aware that you are sick. Otherwise, you will have no motivation for getting well.

The next thing is that the sickness must be acute enough for you to go and see a doctor.

Then, the physician must accurately diagnose the nature of your illness.

Fourth, the physician must prescribe the correct treatment to cure the illness.

Lastly, you must choose to follow the correct treatment in order to be cured.

This is a diagnosis chapter. You have been introduced to the Three Chairs, and you are prepared to look beneath the surface for real insights that have transforming potential for you and the people you love. As you read this chapter, you will understand another of the primary characteristics of each of the Three Chairs. By the end, you will be able to more accurately render a diagnosis on your own life. And, when you have correctly diagnosed yourself, you will be ready to follow a prescription for improving your spiritual health.

FIRST CHAIR: COMMITMENT

Imagine yourself sitting in that First Chair for a moment, even if it is uncomfortable for you. What word would you use to best describe a person who has first-hand faith, someone who sits in this First Chair? Again, the words of Joshua:

"But as for me and my house, we will serve the Lord" (Joshua 24:15b).

These words are not empty of intention for Joshua, either. His words come during the closing season of his life. In the past, he had served the Lord all of his life, he was presently serving the Lord, and he knew he would continue to serve the Lord.

Now that's commitment. That's first-hand faith. Whenever you look at a person who sits in the First Chair, you will always find this type of commitment. So, in your mind, embroider the word "Commitment" into the well-worn fabric of this First Chair. A number of key elements in the committed life of our First Chair role model are evident.

First, the committed freely choose the Lord to be their Lord.

In the same speech where Joshua expresses his commitment to the Lord, he challenges the people to choose the Lord for themselves: "So Joshua said to the people, '...That *you have chosen the Lord for yourselves...*" (Joshua 24:22b). You cannot be committed to something unless you make the initial decision to be committed voluntarily. You need to choose Jesus as your personal Lord. Not just God. Not just Savior. You must take it a step further and willfully pledge yourself to be under His authority and direction. No one can make you take that step except *you*. This commitment is the most important of all the others that follow. Unless you come to this point in your life, you cannot sit in the First Chair for more than a couple of days here and there throughout your Christian life—after a special conference, a mountain top experience, or a traumatic time during which God intervenes and you are trying to express your gratitude. Those are meaningful, to be sure, but sitting in the First Chair goes much deeper. Ultimately, the committed have decided to put their present and future into the hands of the Lord God of heaven because they trust Him.

Early in Joshua's leadership he faced the issue of making this choice for himself. The Lord wanted to revalidate who was ultimately in charge before the Israelites moved in to conquer the Promised Land. Moses was dead. Joshua was now in charge, and God wanted to make sure Joshua would follow Him. Joshua had to choose whether or not to trust and obey God as Lord. He led the people through the miraculous parting of the Jordan River, and they marched through on dry land just as their parents' generation had marched through the Red Sea. They celebrated the Passover and then ate the produce of the Promised Land for the first time—and the next day, the manna disappeared. Forever. God's supply came not one day too late and left not one day too early. Joshua showed himself willing to trust the Lord completely.

Up ahead of the group was the dangerous city of Jericho, with its high and formidable walls. The battle was just about to begin. But when Joshua was close to Jericho, perhaps scouting for the upcoming battle, he looked up, "and behold, a man stood opposite him with his sword drawn in his hand. And Joshua went to him and said to him, 'Are you for us or for our adversaries?'" (Joshua 5:13). Since Joshua was preparing for battle—and the man had his sword drawn—that was an obvious question. But the answer he received was totally unexpected:

"No."

No? How could he not be for one or the other — especially with the drawn sword? The rest of the sentence reads, "As Commander of the army of the Lord I have now come." The next verse captures the spirit of someone who is sitting in the First Chair: "And Joshua fell on his face to the earth and worshipped, and said to him, 'What does my Lord say to His servant?'" Joshua was one of the committed.

He was willing to obey his Lord, come what may. Joshua immediately fell on his face and worshipped. He knew what to do in the presence of God. Joshua also used the words "my Lord" in response. The committed have already decided that Jesus will be their Lord. They have chosen the Lord for themselves. Joshua enlarges this concept in 22:5 when he exhorts the people to "love the Lord your God" and "hold fast to Him." This commitment isn't merely an intellectual one, nor is it simply a volitional one. It is emotional as well—"*love* the Lord your God." It's loyal—"hold fast to Him." The commitment to follow Christ is ongoing and comes from a heart in love with the Lord. The committed see the Lord through the eyes of their love and loyalty. They see the Lord as "my Lord."

Second, the committed wholeheartedly serve the Lord.

Joshua not only saw the Lord as His Lord, but he also saw himself as the Lord's servant. That's the other side of commitment. Joshua put himself into the Lord's trust and charge. He covenanted himself with the Lord in a way similar to the way one spouse vows to the other. When such a commitment is made, it has implications for the person making it. The moment you give yourself to the Lord is the instant you become the Lord's servant. Why? Because the Lord has a plan that involves your direct participation. You are called to His service. To sit in the First Chair, to be one of the committed, means that you are willing to obey His commands.

Everywhere you look, you see the same reaction from the committed. When a person moves into the First Chair, he moves into a completely different mindset. Look again at Joshua's real question: "What does my Lord say to His servant?" (Joshua 5:14c). Joshua is requesting marching orders from his Commander. "*What do you want me to do, Lord?*" The lifelong request of the committed is, "What will You have me to do today?"

Perhaps that's why so many of us who sit in the First Chair wake up with worship in our hearts and that question on our lips. "What would You have me to do today, Lord?" And we close the day with the question, "Well, Lord, how did your servant do today?"

This desire to worship and serve the Lord dwells deep within the soul! Joshua once again exhorts his people in 22:5c: "And to serve Him with all your heart and with all your soul."

To serve Him. With all your heart. With all your soul. That's first hand faith. That's what it is to sit in the First Chair.

Nothing held back when you serve with all your heart.

Nothing held back when you serve with all your soul.

There cannot be any other gods or priorities for the committed. The Lord is Number One. He receives the priority of our love, our effort, our desire, and our energy.

Third, the committed trust and obey the Word of the Lord.

Where do the committed find out what the will of the Lord is? How can they discover what the ways of the Lord are? If they want to serve Him, what does He want done? The Lord knew these same questions were in the heart of Joshua, so at the very beginning of his leadership career, the Lord revealed the requirement for the committed:

> "This Book of the Law shall not depart from your mouth, but you shall meditate on it day and night, that you may observe to do according to all that is written in it. For then you will make your way prosperous, and then you will have good success" (Joshua 1:8).

The Lord wanted His will to be knowable, discernible, and objective, so it was written in the Book of the Law. Whose idea was that? God's. Why? So there could be no mistake, no confusion, and no ignorance of His nature and His will.

What does the Lord promise to those who talk about it ("shall not depart from your mouth"), meditate on it ("you shall meditate on it day and night"), and do it ("that you may observe to do according to all that it is written in it")? He promises that our lives will have incredible results: "For then you will make your way prosperous," the Lord says. "For then you will have good success."

Our culture is fixated on success. Every bookstore is filled with some businessman's latest thoughts on success, and each day thousands of people attend seminars promising to reveal the secrets of success. But there is no "secret" to success. Most people couldn't even give you a good definition of the word, but God has made it clear in the Bible. Draw close to Him, and you'll experience true success.

Joshua wrote a copy of the Law on huge stones, and then he read it to the entire nation—even to the children and the strangers—because the Revelation of God is for all people, no matter what your age or your cultural identity is. Trusting God, serving Him, and allowing Him to be your Lord are the keys to becoming one of the committed. Anyone who wants to be successful according to God's standards must discover the Word of God, and then read, mediate on, talk about, and obey it. That's why Joshua said, "But take diligent heed to *do* the commandment and the law" (Joshua 22:5). If you're going to sit in the First Chair, you're going to have to make a decision to *do* it.

Before we move on to a discussion about the Second Chair, reflect on your life for a moment. Are you one of the committed? Have you chosen the Lord to be *your* Lord? Have you chosen to be His Servant, with all of your heart and all of your soul? Have you put into practice meditating on, talking about, and doing what the Lord has written in the Scriptures? If not, then you may be more comfortable in the Second Chair at this point in your pilgrimage.

SECOND CHAIR: COMPROMISE

The Second Chair person usually starts his spiritual life leaning on the First Chair. If you grew up in a godly home, you were probably pretty close to a First Chair person for several years of your life. Of course, it was not that you actively chose to be there; it was because that was the only life you knew. You recognized your parents' commitment and you modeled your life after theirs. That's the way it should be.

But eventually you have to find a Chair to sit in. In order to sit in the Second Chair, that "parental faith" must become your own "personal faith." As Joshua said, you must choose the Lord for yourself. What you do with the Lord *after* coming to know Him personally determines whether you sit in the First Chair or the Second Chair.

While the word used to describe a person in the First Chair is "committed," the word used to describe a Second Chair person is "compromise." It's interesting that, while the Second Chair person claims to believe all the same truths as someone in the First Chair, he lives nearly identically to someone who is in the Third Chair. The life of compromise and the life of rebellion against God both draw a ridiculous picture when we are talking about a Christian. Imagine someone who is trying to sit in one chair, but who has his arms wrapped around another one. That's the lifestyle a person in the Second Chair is living. At the same time, that individual is trying to get one leg over to the First Chair, just to make sure he's covered all his bases! Does that seem silly? Then you can imagine what God must think when He observes Christians trying to live their lives with one foot in His kingdom and the other in Satan's domain.

You cannot move back to the Third Chair once you are a believer, but you can certainly embrace its lifestyle. You can, however, move from the Third Chair to either the First or Second. Moving into the First Chair means you decide to gain victory in your life, just as Joshua decided to do.

I find it interesting that more Bible scholars have not studied the period of time just after Joshua's speech. When the conquest of Canaan was complete and all the tribes inherited their portion, God fulfilled His promise to Israel: "So the Lord gave to Israel all the land of which He had sworn to give to their fathers, and they took possession of it and dwelt in it. The Lord gave them rest all around, according to all that He had sworn to their fathers. And not a man of all their enemies stood against them; the Lord delivered all their enemies into their hand. Not a word failed of any good thing which the Lord had spoken to the house of Israel. All came to pass" (Joshua 21:43-45).

After the Promised Land was conquered, all that remained was for the individual tribes to completely conquer all parts of their allotted areas. The whole had been conquered by all twelve tribes fighting together, and the battle had been won. And God gave clear command and warning:

"Therefore take diligent heed to yourselves, that you love the Lord your God. Or else, if indeed you do go back, and cling to the remnant of these nations—these that remain among you—and make marriages with them, and go in to them and they to you, know for certain that the Lord your God will no longer drive out these nations from before you. But they shall be snares and traps to you, and scourges on your sides and thorns in your eyes, until you perish from this good land which the Lord your God has given you" (Joshua 23:11-13).

The Book of Judges starts out, right after this, by stating that the twelve tribes were ready to finish the conquest within each of their own territories. "Now after the death of Joshua, it came to pass that the children of Israel asked the Lord, saying, 'Who shall be first to go up for us against the Canaanites to fight against them?'" (Judges 1:1). The time was right. All that Israel had to do was to finish off the remaining tribes and they would have the land God had promised them.

But watch how they slid from commitment to compromise. Israel went from stunning success to shocking defeat. Here are just a few of the recorded statements regarding the battles of the twelve tribes of Israel from Judges Chapter 1:

"Judah could not drive out the inhabitants."

"Benjamin did not drive out the Jebusites."

"Manasseh did not drive out the inhabitants."

"Ephraim did not drive out the Canaanites."

"Zebulun did not drive out the inhabitants."

"Asher did not drive out the inhabitants."

"Naphtali did not drive out the inhabitants."

"The Amorites forced the tribe of Dan into the mountains."

What on earth happened? Commitment bled into compromise. Rather than committing themselves and completing the task they had been given, the twelve tribes decided to take it easy. After all, I'm sure they reasoned, they'd been fighting for a long time. They figured they already had most of the land. They were tired of fighting. Besides, the people who were living there seemed nice enough. So Israel made the choice to not obey God. They compromised on their task. Oh, they said the right words to God, and they made a showing in doing battle with the people of Palestine. But in the end they did not obey the Lord. They were not willing to trust God's plan and obey it. Instead, they listened to what some members of their culture were saying, and decided to compromise.

The compromisers go through the same motions as the committed, but they ultimately do not trust nor obey the Lord.

That's the first principle of the compromisers. When Joshua was in leadership, Israel took the land and not one nation prevailed against them—not one. Even Joshua's last words reminded the "Generation of the Elders" that "the Lord your God will expel them from before you and drive them out of your sight. So you shall possess their land, as the Lord your God has promised you" (Joshua 23:5).

God had promised complete victory, and they had experienced the victory. But they had not become people who were committed to the promises of God at any cost. Even though they had "seen all the great works which He had done for Israel," they had not decided to make God their Lord. They had been through the wilderness, had witnessed the crossing of the Jordan and the defeat of Jericho, had seen years of victory as they conquered nation after nation throughout the Promised Land. But they still had not become committed. What was the difference between Joshua and the Elders who outlived him? Joshua trusted God. The Elders trusted Joshua, who trusted God. They had second-hand faith. Second-hand faith never conquers giants. Second-hand faith never moves mountains! Second-hand faith simply looks at the difficulty of the task and tries to decide if they can accomplish it. First-hand faith looks at the resources of the all-powerful God. Is anything too hard for God?

That's why Joshua tells two of the tribes, "You shall drive out the Canaanites, though they have iron chariots and are strong" (Joshua 17:18b). And yet, when the tribe of Judah does not conquer some of its inheritance, the reason given is "because they had chariots of iron" (Judges 1:19). The committed conquer through their trust in the Lord's power, provision, and promises. The compromisers collapse because of all the reasons victory is impossible.

Joshua's friend Caleb was one of the committed, and he too sat in the First Chair. As the other spy who had joined Joshua in calling for an entrance into the Promised Land, his faith was still undaunted 40 years later. Neither the giants in the land nor the walled cities had frightened Caleb. He wanted to obey the Lord, no matter what. Listen to this man's trust and obedience way back in Numbers 14:9: "Only do not rebel against the Lord nor fear the people of the land, for they are our bread; their protection has departed from them, and the Lord is with us. Do not fear them." Caleb knew the best course of action was to obey the Lord. In the book of Joshua, when Caleb is past 80 years of age, he still has a heart of obedience as he reminisces about the cowardly spies who entered the Land of Canaan with him: "Nevertheless my brethren who went with me made the heart of the people melt, but I wholly followed the Lord my God" (Joshua 14:8).

Those are powerful words of commitment. Caleb knew he had wholly followed the Lord his God. That's the heart of the committed. Do you know what land Caleb wanted? The land with the giants still remaining! Listen to his vibrant faith in the power of the Almighty: "It may be that the Lord will be with me, and I shall be able to drive them out as the Lord said" (Joshua 14:12b). At 85 years of age, Caleb drove out the giants!

What was the difference then, from the enemy they had already conquered and the enemy yet remaining? Absolutely nothing. The difference wasn't in the enemy; it was in the hearts of the people of Israel. The enemy hadn't changed. The people were simply no longer willing to be completely obedient to the Lord. They didn't trust fully in His plan. They could go through the motions as though they were committed, but when it came down to it, they wanted to compromise.

Compromisers disobey God for personal pleasure and possessions.

What happened when the tribes of Israel grew in size so that they were powerful "without the Lord"—that is, they could defeat the enemy in their own strength? They stopped thinking about God. Here's the summary verse: "And it came to pass, when Israel was strong, that they put the Canaanites under tribute, but did not completely drive them out" (Judges 1:28).

The Lord had given them such explicit commands and warnings regarding driving out and destroying the Canaanites, but they didn't follow through because they had not chosen to have the Lord be *their* Lord. They weren't strong enough to obey the Lord without seeing those remarkable first-hand miracles and answers to prayer. Instead, they disobeyed God so that they could make money from their enemies. Covetousness became the god of the compromisers. They liked what disobedience could give to them more than what obedience would. Disobedience allowed them to have slaves, money from tribute, and foreign women. Their desire for pleasure and possessions was stronger than their love for the Lord. That's what Joshua was concerned about when he warned the second generation that "they should love the Lord...or else, if indeed you do go back, and cling to the remnant of these nations..." (Joshua 23:11b-12a). The root issue was simple: did they love the Lord completely, or did they love the things of the world more?

This was not an isolated problem, either. A quick glance through Judges Chapter 1 reveals that Zebulun put the Canaanites under tribute, Naphtali put the inhabitants under tribute, and Dan put the Amorites under tribute. Everybody wanted to get a piece of the action. They claimed that they had won a hard-fought victory, but they hadn't obeyed the Lord. They had compromised. They went through motions, but they ultimately did not trust Him enough to do what He said. They put their own personal pleasure ahead of God's plan.

Compromisers accept the values and lifestyles of the Third Chair.

The farther compromisers move away from commitment, the more they inevitably identify with the values of the Third Chair culture that surrounds them. They have no internal strength from conviction birthed out of commitment, and so they vacillate. In time, the lifestyles of those Second Chair people look identical to those in the Third Chair. Tragically, the offspring of the Second Chair people become one with the people of the land and never meet the Lord. That's why Judges Chapter 1 notes, "The Jebusites dwell with the children of Benjamin," "the Canaanites dwelt in Gezer among the people of Ephraim," "the Canaanites dwelt among the tribe of Zebulun," "the Asherites dwelt among the Canaanites...for they did not drive them out," and "Naphtali dwells among the Canaanites."

When the litany of such defeat and discouragement is complete, Judges Chapter 2 opens as the Angel of the Lord offers Israel a sobering statement of judgment: "I led you up from Egypt and brought you to the land of which I swore to your fathers; and I said, 'I will never break My covenant with you. And you shall make no covenant with the inhabitants of this land; you shall tear down their altars.' But you have not obeyed my voice. Why have you done this? Therefore I also said, 'I will not drive them out before you, but they shall be thorns in your side, and their gods shall be a snare to you" (Judges 2:2b-3).

The elders who outlived Joshua knew the Lord, and they knew of all His great works. Yet they rejected God and His Will for them. Instead of driving out the remaining enemy, they made covenants with the inhabitants, in direct disobedience to God. They did not tear down the altars of false gods, even though they had been told explicitly to do so. As I studied this, I wondered, "Did the people of Israel realize their disobedience, or was the angel's judgment news to them?" I got my answer Judges 2:4: "So it was, when the Angel of the Lord spoke these words to all the children of Israel, that the people lifted up their voice and wept...and they sacrificed there to the Lord." Not only had they compromised on the direct word of God, but *they knew they were doing it all along.* A person in the Chair of compromise always knows he is living in disobedience, but he never believes that God will judge his life or his family for the sin. Had Israel left the Lord? No, not at all. They still believed in Him. That's why they sacrificed to Him. They knew His Word was true— they just didn't want to obey it. They preferred to compromise with the world.

There is one other tragic element in this story. Maybe the nation of Israel *had* done wrong and knew it. Maybe they did weep and sacrifice. And maybe they did ask God to forgive them, and pleaded with Him not to bring judgment to them. But they did not repent and then obey the Lord by turning right around and driving out their enemy. They could easily have done so. They were too used to compromising to do anything so distasteful as that! They liked the slaves, felt they needed the money, and didn't see what harm a few pagan temples could do.

You see, the people in the Second Chair were so deeply committed to themselves that, even with an open verbal rebuke and promise of strong judgment from the very Angel of the Lord, they would not submit. They could have, but they did not. A few of them remained obedient to God. Caleb was one, and there were no doubt others. Thank the Lord that some do!

THIRD CHAIR: CONFLICT

When you grow up in a home that knows the Lord but doesn't honor Him as Lord, a home that compromises throughout life in many private and public ways, it affects you. It shapes you. You can't help but be troubled by internal conflict. "If this God stuff is so important," you reason, "why don't they obey it at all times?" You may see your parents weep over tragedies in their lives, but you do not see them make substantial changes reflecting true commitment to Christ. Your parents "dwell among them" and "make a covenant with" the world, and even permit its "altars" to remain. But you grew up without having seen Joshua do great works, or even hearing of what it was like to have a life of commitment.

The conflict generation doesn't know the Lord or His works.

Remember the description of people in the Third Chair from Judges 2:10: "When all that generation had been gathered to their fathers, another generation arose after them who did not know the Lord nor the work which He had done for Israel." The Third Chair is filled with people who don't even know about God, for they've never seen the power of God on display in anyone's life.

People of the first generation have long passed out of memory....

People of the second generation are either dead or very old....

And the people of the third generation do not know the Lord.

What does all this mean in practical terms? The offspring of the compromiser generation frequently do not come to know the Lord—or if they do, it is in spite of their parents and usually at a distant location from them. The offspring of the compromiser don't even know of the heritage of their own families. They don't know where they have come from, what they believe, or why they believe it. The third generation becomes filled with conflict, wondering why their parents serve a God who seems distant to them. The generation that came after the elders were the same way.

The conflict generation worships and serves the gods of the land.

This description is just as scary. You see, the people in the Third Chair just grew up in their culture. In the midst of the society they found themselves... "among them." Like them. Their parents had some religious practices which, at times, seemed out of touch with reality and a bit of a pain in the neck. So what does a person in the Third Chair do in such a situation, where even the knowledge of the reality of God and His past works are absent? You join with the people of the land. You become one of the crowd. Unfortunately, the crowd doesn't know God. They do, however, know of other gods: Baal in Canaan, Spirit Guides in America, Ashtoreths in the mountains of Canaan, Satanic worship among some of the major rock stars of our country. Whether it's tribute from their enemies or selling out for the "American Dream," the people in the Third Chair worship other gods. Only the names change. The principle remains the same.

A generation that knows the Lord but doesn't remain loyal to Him (those in the Second Chair) will inevitably produce a generation that doesn't know the Lord and turns to serve the gods of the land (those in the Third Chair). I don't know how you perceive the Christians in the United States, but after 25 years of ministry there is absolutely no doubt in my mind that most of them have embraced the world's culture; most of them are Second Chair Christians. There is no real difference in the values and lifestyles of those people in the church and those outside the church. They experience the same percentage of divorces and they have the same level of immorality. They have the same everything.

I can already hear a complaint echoing through the land: "But those people really don't know the Lord." May I differ with you? I believe many of them do indeed know the Lord and trust Jesus Christ for their eternal salvation. Unfortunately, the Christian masses of this nation are sitting in the Second Chair and leaning so far toward the Third Chair that we can barely identify where they sit except by asking them questions!

And their offspring are, by and large, snuggled down deep in the seat of the Third Chair. Do you realize what kind of generation is being raised? I use that term very loosely since most of the kids these days are not being raised by anyone—they are usually either "latchkey kids" who come home to an empty house because their parent or parents are working, or they are children in a home with non-involved parents. Our country, tragically, is raising a whole generation of those who do not know the Lord, nor do they know the works that He has done. We call this the secularization of America, and for all intents and purposes, it's almost complete.

The conflict generation becomes one with its society.

What happened in the lives of this third generation in the second chapter of Judges? I'll give you a sampling, but you can read it in more detail for yourself: "The children of Israel did evil in the sight of the Lord," "they served the Baals," "they forsook the Lord God of their fathers," "they followed other gods from among the gods of the people who were all around," "they bowed down to them," and "they provoked the Lord to anger." When that third generation grew up, they rejected the true God and became one with the pagan society around them.

How did God respond? "He delivered them into the hands of the plunderers who despoiled them; and He sold them into the hands of their enemies all around, so that they could no longer stand before their enemies...And they were greatly distressed...they did not cease from their own doings nor from their stubborn way" (Judges 2:14, 15, 19). He also sent judges to deliver them from their distresses, "for the Lord was moved to pity by their groaning because of those who oppressed them and harassed them." There was conflict everywhere. Conflict would sometimes bring them back to the Lord because of His enduring mercy and compassion, but the people did not truly repent and return to the First Chair, or even to the Second Chair. Instead, they got even more involved with their culture.

"So the children of Israel dwelt among the Canaanites, the Hittites, the Amorites, the Perizzites, the Hivites, and the Jebusites. And they took their daughters to be their wives, and gave their daughters to be their sons; and they served their gods. So the children of Israel did evil in the sight of the Lord. They forgot the Lord their God, and served the Baals and Asherahs" (Judges 3:5-7).

Their children lived among the nations, to the degree that they fully intermarried with those who did not know the Lord nor His works, served their false gods, and did evil in the sight of the Lord. Conflict is in every direction for those who chose to sit in the Third Chair. They had internal conflicts over their parents' faith, external conflict with the surrounding nations, and eternal conflict as they tried to right themselves with God. Conflict internally, externally, and eternally—that is the description of the third generation after Joshua. And this is compelling reason to flee the Third Chair.

This chapter intended to move you into a diagnosis of what ails you. Later chapters will present and explore the lives of those three generations even deeper, and they will offer recommended treatment. But before moving on, do you have a clear sense of where you sit in these chairs? The following chart can help you clarify each of the three Chairs.

The First Chair	The Second Chair	The Third Chair
"Joshua"	"The Elders"	"Another Generation"
Commitment	Compromise	Conflict
Knows God personally	Knows God personally	Knows not God personally
#1 Chooses the Lord to be his/her Lord	#1 Looks like committed but does not trust or obey	#1 Doesn't know God or His works
#2 Wholeheartedly serves the Lord	#2 Disobeys God for personal pleasure and possessions	#2 Worships and serves the gods of the land
#3 Trusts and obeys the Word of the Lord	#3 Accepts the values and lifestyles of the Third Chair—full tolerance as if equally acceptable	#3 Becomes one with the society
Christ as Lord	Christ as Savior	Christ as religious leader

STUDY QUESTIONS

1. How would you describe the commitment of the first generation?

2. How does the second generation compromise?

3. Why is the third generation marked by conflict?

4. How do you see yourself compromising with the world in a way your parents did not?

5. Does that bother you? Why or why not?

CHAPTER FIVE

From Compromise to Commitment

This chapter has one clear and unmistakable goal: to enable you to move from the Second Chair to the First Chair in your level of commitment to the Lord. If you already consider yourself to be a First Chair person, then this chapter will affirm your decision and move you even further down that road of total commitment to Christ.

Unlike the previous chapters, this chapter will be much more personal, as if we were talking person to person, just as if you were sitting in our den having a comfortable conversation about your desire to become more committed to Christ. I take it for granted that, since you have continued reading this far into this book, you would like to know more of the truth that will set you free to become the committed Christian you know the Lord would like you to be. So, let's get started.

THE TRUTH ABOUT COMPROMISE AND COMMITMENT

Consider the *"Continuum of Commitment"* on the next page. Take a moment to locate yourself in one of those numbered boxes.

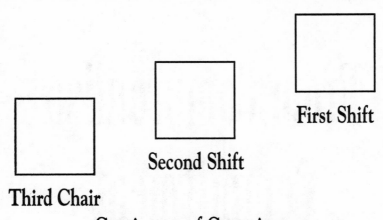

First Shift

Second Shift

Third Chair

Continuum of Commitment

Put a "T" in the box that best describes what would be true about your level of commitment during the past 12 months. That "T" stands for "Today." Now reflect back five years from today. Think about where you were living, where you were working, your involvement with your local church, your patterns of personal holiness, your discipline in your walk with the Lord, and your level of commitment at that point in your life. Use the number "5" to mark the spot you were five years ago, and then do the same for ten years ago using the number "10."

What would you say is the trend of the last decade of your life? Would you say you are heading in the right direction? Making solid progress? Stuck in a rut? Way out of line? What best describes your spiritual walk these past ten years?

Now I'd like you to do one more thing. In one of the boxes, put the letter "G" for the goal you have regarding the level of commitment you want to see in your life by the end of this year. Now you have a sense of where you've been, where you are today, and where you want to be in the future.

There is probably some territory to cover between now and then, and no single step will span it. It probably won't be a simple as rolling down a hill. Instead, there are some areas of challenge and some difficulties that lie between your present position and your future goal. But that is the whole point of having a goal—to cover new territory and move ahead. I have had conversations about spiritual progress innumerable times in the past. Do you know what I discovered? Most people have never given much thought to the issues that stand in the way of making significant progress to a deeper commitment. When I ask for them to list the things they need to do, they struggle for a few minutes, considering possibilities. Inevitably, however, it comes down to between three and five things that they'd like to change. Their answers usually include one or two sizable problems, and a few relatively minor issues. In other words, there are usually only a handful of roadblocks that stand in the way of a person reaching his goal. Christian maturity is the same way. If a person can name the roadblocks and create a plan for overcoming those roadblocks, he's well on his way to sitting in the First Chair.

What are the five roadblocks in your life, as you see them, that keep you from maturity? There may be more than five, but typically there are not. Now, in each of the boxes below, write a word or two that expresses each roadblock in your spiritual life, using the size box that represents how difficult the problem feels to you.

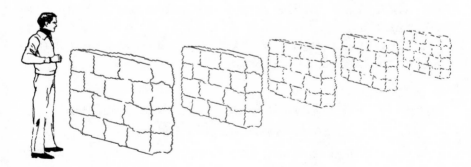

Unfortunately, most of our lives are spent doing everything except a little self-examination, and you may not be used to doing this kind of thinking. Mark Twain once suggested, "Take out your brain and jump on it—it gets all caked up!" So after you've jumped on your brain a bit, you should be able to form a fairly clear picture of your situation—past, present, and future—and the obstacles you face.

Now for the pay-off: people who are undeniably committed to Christ all know and experience certain key elements in their Christian pilgrimage. I have discovered four distinct resources for gaining God's wisdom:

First, I can turn to the commands and principles in the Scriptures.

Second, I can examine the lives of the Old and New Testament saints.

Third, I can mimic the lives of outstanding Christian saints.

Fourth, I can remember the lessons the Lord has taught my family, my friends, and myself.

Separated, the first resource listed is the most reliable, and the fourth is the least reliable. But, by far, the most effective plan of all is when all four resources are used together. That is, you have experienced what the Bible directly teaches and what it indirectly illustrates, you know what the normal experience of great Christians throughout history has been. I said before that there are no "secrets" in getting into the First Chair. But if there were any, these would be the best places to look for them.

THE FIVE TRANSFORMATIONAL TRUTHS OF THE COMMITTED

Every serious Christian wants to get into the First Chair, and most of us know that the committed life means having a mature walk with Jesus Christ. But some people are still waiting to find the "secret" to maturity. I have a surprise for you.

The "secrets" all have to do with what you believe!

Any obstacle, including what you wrote in the boxes above, exists only because of you believe that a lie is true. A lie tells you that you aren't busy enough, sensitive enough, or smart enough to be truly spiritual. But the moment you understand the corresponding truth, you can renounce the lie immediately. It will no longer make sense to you. The moment you no longer believe a lie is the same moment it no longer has any power over you. You can replace it with the truth of the Scriptures, which draws us like a powerful magnet toward Jesus Christ.

Lies keep us in bondage; they cause us to stop or to retreat. Truth frees us from that bondage; it causes us to start again, moving toward maturity. To believe a lie means that we do not believe the corresponding truth—enslaved, because we behave according to what we believe. Our behavior is the out-working of our belief. That's why you cannot change your behavior while accepting the lie that caused you to behave in the first place. When you start to re-direct your thinking onto truth, consciously or subconsciously your heart tells you that this new behavior really won't be the smartest or the best behavior. But if you can really change what you believe, you will find your previous behavior unacceptable. You wouldn't *want* to continue doing the same things that you want to change–and you *wouldn't* continue doing them!

There is a phrase in the business community for this change in the way you think about something. It's called a "paradigm shift." Believing one paradigm, or set of truths that define a given situation, paralyzes you and keeps you from embracing another. For example, if you believe that a church should be organized congregationally, with every believer having an equal say in matters of policy, you'll struggle with the way churches in many Hispanic countries are organized. Many of those view the church from a completely different perspective. They would say that a church is not an organization at all, that it is a relationship. People don't "vote" in relationships; they come to agreement. For you to embrace that perspective, your paradigm of church organization would need to be altered significantly. I'm not saying that in this case one perspective is right while the other is wrong. What I am saying is that in order to understand something in a new way, there must be some sort of a paradigm shift.

But before the business community ever considered a "paradigm shift," the Bible taught the principle of rejecting lies and embracing truth. Its term is even more accurate. The term used in the New Testament is *metanoia*. *Metanoia* is a compound word: *meta* means "after," and *noia* means "to think" or "consider." *Metanoia* means that a person thinks differently after either a verbal or experiential instruction. If you've ever said something like, "When the professor explained that, the light went on for me. I'll never be able to go back to my old way of thinking after that!" That's a *metanoia* response to verbal instruction. What about, "Boy, did I ever learn I lesson from that–I'll never do that again for as long as I live"? That's a *metanoia* response to experiential instruction. When that *metanoia* occurred, a total change of thought took place as it reached down into your heart. When a person's heart has truly been changed, then his habits soon follow.

Have you connected the English word we use to translate *metanoia* yet? It's "repentance." You see, the Bible knows that if a person truly believes differently, then he will behave differently. That's why Jesus Christ said, "He that has ears to hear, let him hear." Everyone around Him was hearing the words He was speaking, but too few of them were really hearing the message. What did Christ mean? Only that if you really heard what He said, you would experience a repentance of mind and heart, and your behavior would come into line with that.

So if you changed, becoming more committed to Christ, how would *we* know it? That's right—your behavior would reflect it. In other words, you would behave in a more committed way. And what would have to happen first for you to behave in a more committed way? Right, again—your beliefs must change. If your beliefs become more committed, your behavior follows.

Now, go back to your five boxes. If my hunch is correct, the obstacles you wrote in were all *behaviors* you want changed, not *beliefs* you want changed! Be honest: how many times have you tried to change those behaviors already without any lasting success? Well, you now know why! You failed not from a lack of desire but from a lack of "repentance," a lack of a shift in your thinking. In other words, you tried to change what you did before you changed what you thought. And, except for rare instances, that doesn't work.

Therefore, what must be the "secret" of those people who are sitting in the First Chair, growing more and more committed to Christ? They had *metanoia* instruction in some form. What they believed before they renounced as being untrue. When they chose to believe what the truth really was and embraced that, their behavior came into full agreement. The Bible calls that whole process "repentance."

When was the last time you repented? If you haven't had identifiable "repentances" in the last twelve months, then you have probably been stalled right where you are for quite a while, perhaps even retreating farther away from the First Chair. Now here's something that sounds odd: in the past ten years, I have had a repentance about repentance! Previously, I didn't look at repentance as a particularly valuable or attractive concept. Now, though, it is one of my most valued concepts. And why is that? Because I have learned from both the Bible and experience that I cannot grow spiritually if I just repent of the behaviors I don't want. Without specific acts of repentance regarding what I believe, the behaviors that result from those beliefs won't change.

What a reversal! Now, it is my personal pattern to find unbiblical actions and attitudes in my life. I follow their threads back into my heart and mind to find the unbiblical beliefs that serve as their root systems. Then, it's off to the Bible and some rather tough soul-searching as I seek the Lord's illumination into the error in my thinking. I tear down those false thought processes (called "strongholds" by Paul) with the truth of Scriptures. I focus on filling my mind with the truth of God, and rejecting the lies and deceit of Satan. Finally, I repent by confession of those related sinful acts and attitudes, and I renounce those behavior patterns.

What freedom! What liberty! I can finally experience victory because the internal root system that keeps me in bondage to the lie has been ripped out. Instead of the lies, there is an internal commitment to the truth. The truth always sets us free to do what our inner spiritual man encourages us to do.

We can even go one step further: since the root of your behavior is always what you believe, the problem is never what you are doing—that is merely the *fruit on the tree*. The only way to get rid of the bad fruit you don't want any more is not to frantically pick it all off in one moment of emotionalism. It will only reappear at a later time. You need, rather, to dig right down into the root system below the surface. That is what gives life to the fruit. Pull up the root and the fruit cannot support itself.

So, once again, go back to your boxes. Since we've seen that each behavior is a result of the lie under the surface, that is what we need to find. Nobody knowingly believes a lie. You believe something because you think it is the truth. But whatever is supporting the behavior you want to see changes is, most definitely, a lie. It must be. Truth only produces a life of holiness and commitment. A life lacking in holiness and commitment comes only from *not* believing the truth.

When you meet a truly committed believer, someone who is sitting in the First Chair, you can be absolutely sure of one thing: he believes a great deal of truth. In fact, I think it would be safe to say that the more truth a person believes, the more committed he will be. How incredibly liberating! We do not have to be in the dark regarding how to go about this lifelong process of being more and more conformed to the image of Jesus Christ. It's encouraging, isn't it, that we do not have to experience defeat after defeat without knowing why? We can know the truth, and the truth will set us free.

The Bible speaks of two alternatives for your commitment: either you commit to the Lord and His Kingdom, or you commit to the world and its values. The more deeply committed a person is to something, the more he becomes like that thing. A football player who is deeply committed to a coach begins to think about the game like his coach does. We become like the people to which we are committed because we respect their opinions; we become like the things to which we are committed because we respect what they stand for. The Bible, therefore, describes our relationship to what or whom we respect by saying that we are either "conformed to the image of His Son" or "conformed to the world." According to the Bible, we were all fully conformed to the world, buying into its values and practices—that is, we were before we met Jesus. When we come to know the Lord, we start a lifelong journey in the opposite direction. We are in the process not of *conforming* to the world, but of being *transformed* into what God would have us be—like His Son. And we want to be like Him because we respect who He is and what He stands for.

The question before you, then, is this: are you absolutely sure that a change in thinking is the only way to experience transformation into a person is more committed to the Lord and His will for your life?" God's Truth is absolutely reliable. Read slowly and consider it carefully:

> "And do not be conformed to this world, but be transformed by the renewing of your mind, that you may prove what is that good and acceptable and perfect will of God" (Romans 12:2).

Everything that we have discussed is directly related to this truth; this verse is packed with insight for those who want to sit in the First Chair.

"AND DO NOT BE CONFORMED TO THIS WORLD"

The Lord does not want any of His people conforming to the world because the world is directly opposed to Him and His ways. Paul is clear in this letter to the believers who lived in Rome: don't do something that you can do just to show off. Don't allow yourself to continue to be poured into the mold of the world. People who know the Lord and who are still conformed to this world in some significant way are people who compromise—people who sit in the Second Chair. People who are conformed to the image of Jesus Christ are the committed ones in the First Chair.

"BUT BE TRANSFORMED"

Transformation is the process of "not being conformed to this world but being conformed to the image of the Lord." Being conformed to that image is synonymous with our main theme of being fully committed. The more conformed you are to the Lord's image, the more committed you are to Him. The more committed you are to the Lord, the more conformed you are to His image.

The word that Paul used when he wrote about being "transformed" is a fascinating one. It comes from the word "metamorphosis," which means to change from one form to another. In a sense, Paul is saying that you can be formed around the world or you can be formed around the Lord Jesus Christ. It's one or the other, and the mature Christian chooses to be shaped into the likeness of his Lord. And, of course, "metamorphosis" is the same thing that occurs between the caterpillar stage and the butterfly stage. It's incredible, isn't it, that our Creator God made something so fat, slow, with a million legs, ugly, and anything but delicate, and then lets that thing change into something that is slender, fast, extraordinarily delicate, and with wings so splendid in color? It's almost as if He wanted to demonstrate the extreme transformation that is possible when He is involved. Nothing is impossible with God.

How does a caterpillar's body transform into that of a butterfly? You won't find much inside its cocoon. But when it's done, stand back. The same is true of a person who gives his life to Jesus. A man who was conformed to the world can be transformed into a committed man of God—sold out to heaven rather than earth, living life abundantly, and serving God with all of his heart, mind, soul, and body. How does that happen? That's in the next part of the verse.

"BY THE RENEWING OF YOUR MIND"

Since Jesus rose from the dead, making new life possible for us, the key to a changed life is in the mind. It's what you think, what you believe, that shapes how you live—changing your beliefs, not changing your behavior. That's why putting your focus on the behaviors in your five boxes will never set you free for transformation. And that's why the vast majority of Christians through history have never sat in the First Chair. Either they don't know or they choose not to believe that God has told us how transformation happens: "by the renewing of your mind." Every time you renew your mind, you turn from one thought to embrace a different thought. You turn from a thought that wasn't true and to a thought that is. You renounce a lie and rely on the truth. In other words, every time you experience a "renewing of your mind," you go through the process of we talked about earlier—repentance.

Then when do those problems in your boxes get taken care of? Well, they change during the process. As your mind is renewed, your thinking changes. You begin believing the truth, and that affects your behavior. You won't respond to people the same way anymore. You won't think about yourself the same way. As your mind is renewed, your life begins to change.

"THAT YOU MAY PROVE"

Another thing Paul points out is that, as your mind is renewed, you are going to prove something to someone: you will prove something to yourself. The word "prove" basically means to prove something experientially, not mentally. So, you do something mentally so that you "prove" in practice. And what is it that you experience as you renew your mind? That's what the last part of the verse is all about.

"WHAT IS THAT GOOD AND ACCEPTABLE AND PERFECT WILL OF GOD."

Dust off your grammar for a moment so we can isolate the essence of what this verse is really teaching. After the word "is" are the words "good and acceptable and perfect." All of those words are adjectives; they describe the person, place, or thing they are connected to. These three words describe the next phrase: "will of God." So the complete thought, without adjectives, is, "What is that will of God."

As your mind is renewed, you are going to prove something experientially to yourself about what the will of God is. You're going to prove to yourself through your own experience that the will of God is *good* in your sight, is *acceptable* to you, and is absolutely *perfect*. That experience will serve as an incredible pull toward the will of God in future situations. Every time you renew your mind a little more, your experience will change.

I think that you will be absolutely shocked, amazed at how wonderful things turn out when you are doing the will of God. Life is still hard, but at least you will know that you are on track. And, more and more, you will *want* the will of God for your life. Everything else will be the complete opposite—bad, imperfect, and unpleasant. You will become more and more convinced of that, not only in your mind but also in your experience. The things that you compromised on earlier in your life, the ways in which you conformed to the world and its values, won't bring you joy, liberty, love, and fulfillment.

Right now, you might not be sure that the Lord's ways will bring those things either, so why bother to change? But if you are willing to start the process, if you are willing to renew your mind, you *will* find out that the Lord's will *is* good every single time, in every place, in every situation, with every person. And it will help to remind yourself that what you have experienced through your previous compromises is the very opposite of good. Things might even have been incredibly bad.

You will also find God's will for your life becoming "acceptable" to you, from your new perspective. You won't have to worry about God's will being merely "satisfactory"; you'll find it fulfilling and pleasing beyond all measure.

You will also find that the will of God is flawless. It's perfect.

Experience will prove to you that His ways cannot be improved upon. More and more often, you will stop trying to out-guess God. Finally, knowing that His will is perfect, you will be liberated to start believing the truth that you have been fighting for so many years. The Lord's ways will be perfect in your sight because you will have experienced the results of doing life His way—and those results are without equal. God's ways are above and beyond; they are incredibly wonderful.

That's why, when you find a person who is truly committed to the Lord, he is continuing to grow more and more like Jesus Christ. Everything that he has learned and everything that he has experienced has overwhelmed him with unspeakable joy. He knows God. And who would ever want to go back from there? Certainly not a person who has sat in the First Chair!

1. What words best described your spiritual life ten years ago? Five years ago? Now?

2. Where would you like to be in your walk with Christ in one year?

3. After reading this chapter, what would you say is holding you back? Why?

4. How do beliefs control behaviors?

5. How does a Christian go about renewing his or her mind?

CHAPTER SIX

The Secrets
of the
Committed
Part One

Something I've learned in life is that the basics always rule. Every successful basketball coach I've ever known emphasized the basics. He begins with dribbling, passing, shooting stances, and good footwork on defense. Good coaches don't start with fancy backdoor passes or spinning slams; they focus on the basics. And nine times out of ten, a team that is good at the basics will beat a team of undisciplined players trying to rely on fancy footwork and exceptional plays.

A good football coach is the same way. He focuses on blocking, tackling, and carrying the football. He knows that games are won with good blocking and tackling, not with flawless execution of the "flea-flicker." Again, the basics rule. The Super Bowl is played in America each year, and what determines the ultimate victory of the champions, more than any other factor, is that they were more skilled in the use of the basics. You can look it up. The team that blocked better, tackled better, and held onto the football usually won the game. They've practiced the same things over and over again. What didn't control the outcome of the most advanced football teams in the world were fancy plays with multiple intricate steps.

This truth about basics is operative everywhere—from football to heart surgery, from public speaking to writing a best seller. That's why the pros practice the basics all the time, over and over. Correct understanding and application of the basics controls the outcome. Learn the basics of anything and you can master 80 percent of the whole. And if you really want to be successful, don't stop at learning the basics; become skilled in the use of them. The basics are what determine winners. If you can figure out the relationship between the basics and your goals, and you'll discover how to use a system to accomplish your objectives.

During the past ten years, Walk Thru the Bible has trained more Christian teachers on the basics of teaching than just about anyone else in the world, and we have discovered what makes a teacher extraordinary. An extraordinary teacher uses the basics of how to cause the students to learn with understanding and skill, and he uses them over and over again. Whenever I am brought into a situation and asked to help a floundering teacher, I always discover that they're neglecting the basics. In fact, I have yet to meet the first exception. Teachers do not fail because of a lack of knowledge, or a lack of caring, or from a lack of desire. They fail simply because they do not understand and apply the basics of teaching. The universal principles involved in causing a person to learn are operative and effective for any teacher, for any subject, and for any group of students. A whole school can be spiraling downward, everyone throwing their hands up in despair over the lack of discipline and the plummeting test scores; but when one "master teacher" arrives, suddenly all the "impossibles" and "you just don't know my students" seem to disappear. What changed? Simply one or two human beings who understood the basics and used them effectively.

If you want to become a First Chair Christian, one who is truly committed to Christ, then you need to realize that spiritual maturity isn't some vast, complicated, intricate, mysterious, or indefinable thing. And the committed are not born with any unique traits like a greater intelligence, a better physical appearance, or any special intuition.

Stop a moment: do you really believe what I just said? Or do you still hold onto the false concept that the committed have something in them that you don't have in yourself, that it's just too complicated for you. Well, why would you believe that the basics rule everything else but not *this* all-important issue? So perhaps it's time to tell yourself the truth: if you are still sitting in the Second Chair while talking about how much you want to be in the First Chair, either you do not know the basics, or you do not practice them.

In this chapter, we will talk about what the basics are for life in the First Chair. The basics are what we believe to be true; they are what make up our paradigm. Therefore, the basics are always beliefs and not behaviors. As we choose to believe, so we choose to behave. Listed below are the six primary beliefs of the committed. I think they are at the root of most of the behaviors that we all want to see at work in the life of a person who is truly committed to the Lord.

BASIC RULE #1:

IF YOU WANT TO BE MATURE, CHANGE YOUR BELIEF ABOUT THE FOCUS OF YOUR COMMITMENT.

When you hear the words "being committed," what do you think about? What is commitment? Who is going to be the recipient of your commitment? Are you going to be committed to Christianity as a religion? Are you going to be committed to your local church as a group of people? Will it mean you are going to be committed to certain behaviors, such as devotions or tithing or sharing your faith? Does it mean you are going to be committed to becoming a missionary or a full-time Christian worker? How are you going to be committed to your spouse and family?

All those questions are important, but being committed to any of those will not necessarily make you a truly committed person. Even having "daily devotions" will not make you a committed person; many people practice this discipline and still are not First Chair Christians. These behaviors are not the *root*; they are the *fruit* of commitment. They are *behaviors* that may or may not help your commitment. Friend, if you focus on any of the things listed above, worthy as they may be, you will never become the committed person you want to be. In fact, those activities may be the very barriers that keep you from total commitment to Christ, because they are not *Him*. The committed have a single focus to their commitment: Jesus Christ. Their commitment is not to the Bible, the church, or Christian service; it is not to anything or anyone except Jesus. Right where you are, say His name. If you are in a crowded place, whisper it under your breath repeatedly and shout it toward heaven in your heart. Jesus! He is the focus of our commitment.

The committed are simply loyal to Jesus. The committed simply follow Jesus. The committed simply obey Jesus. The committed simply submit to Jesus. The committed would die for Jesus. The committed would give anything for Jesus at any time and for any reason. The committed live their lives for Jesus. The committed are sold out to Jesus. The committed simply love Jesus. Friend, love Jesus! Focus on Jesus and your commitment will flourish. Focus on Jesus and your behavior will be revolutionized.

Do you feel comfortable with those words or do they make you a bit uneasy? They may very well make you uncomfortable if your soul is at war. Who controls your life: Jesus or yourself? The Spirit of God who dwells within you is always active when Jesus is lifted up. You see, the Spirit always seeks to glorify Christ in your heart and through your behavior. That troubles all the false gods that lie hidden beneath the surface of your thoughts. Jesus will have no other gods before Him. Although you may never have thought about it, your heart may be filled with many other things that come before Him. The committed have no other gods before Jesus; the compromisers have many other gods before Him. Unfortunately, the more religious a person is, the more the gods in his life are religious, and the harder they can be to identify.

Once you experience salvation, you have the privilege of walking with Him for the rest of your physical life as well as receiving eternal life. And your life will be full of many and varied choices about who He is going to be in relationship to everything and everyone else. He invites you to put everything and everyone in second place, behind Him. Anything else you might choose needs to be so far behind Him that it will look like there is nothing else on the horizon of your life except Jesus.

Just Jesus.

The committed people who sit in the First Chair have decided to follow Jesus. He is all there is.

As we follow Him, He Himself will lead us to forsake all other goals and set aside all other agendas. Those moments of choice—choosing to put Him first—are what I call the *moments of destiny for the committed*. Don't be mistaken. Those moments can be years of intense, even fierce personal struggle. Letting go of your personal agenda is perhaps the hardest thing you will ever do. But until you let go of whatever is in your hand, your hand cannot open to find the hand of Jesus.

Is this complicated, complex, or confusing? Not a bit. It's one of the basics of the committed, and it can be boiled down into just two words: *choose Jesus*.

Now if you turn your heart to the Word of God and listen to the words of Jesus with humility, you will never be confused about or unsure whether that is exactly what He asks of you today. He said, "If anyone desires to come after Me, let him deny himself, and take up his cross, and follow me. For whoever desires to save his life will lose it, and whoever loses his life for My sake will find it" (Matthew 16:24-25). In another place, the Lord said, "If anyone comes to Me, and does not hate his father and mother, wife and children, brothers and sisters, yes, and his own life also, he cannot be My disciple. And whoever does not bear his cross and come after Me cannot be My disciple. So likewise, whoever of you does not forsake all that he has cannot be My disciple" (Luke 14:26, 27, &33). And in John 12:24-26, He said, "Most assuredly, I say to you, unless a grain of wheat falls into the ground and dies, it remains alone; but if it dies, it produces much grain. He who loves his life will lose it, and he who hates his life in this world will keep it for eternal life. If anyone serves Me, let him follow Me; and where I am, there My servant will be also. If anyone serves Me, him My Father will honor."

The central issue is to follow Him. Choose Jesus. When Paul wrote of his life focus, he knew that choosing Jesus is at the heart of the Christian life, and that it is the most strategic choice for the believer: "But what things were gain to me, these I have counted loss for Christ. But indeed I also count all things loss *for the excellence of the knowledge of Christ Jesus my Lord,* for whom I have suffered the loss of all things, count them as rubbish, that I may gain Christ...that I may know Him, and the power of His resurrection, and the fellowship of His sufferings, being conformed to His death" (Philippians 3:7, 8, 10).

Why don't the majority of people who "know the Lord" and "know about His works," those who sit in the Second Chair, choose to be First Chair followers of Jesus Christ? Why do they choose a life of compromise and never experience the reality of life with Him. Why do they choose to forego a dynamic, incredible first-hand faith? The Bible has an answer that may surprise you.

Ultimately, Second Chair people remain in the Second Chair and never break free from compromise to enter the joy of commitment because of what they believe. About what? About Jesus. Simple, isn't it? Put directly, *Second Chair people believe somewhere deep inside that, for them, the best thing is not to commit fully to Jesus.*

No one knowingly chooses to believe a lie. If a Second Chair person really believed the truth about who Jesus is and what that means to mankind, he would become committed right this instant. *First Chair people believe somewhere deep inside that, for them, the best thing is to commit fully to Jesus.* The only difference is the word "not." They believe that Jesus is the person to whom they should fully commit themselves and whom they should serve with all their hearts, souls, and minds. Second Chair people believe a lie about one of the following: the person of the Lord, the power of the Lord, the purpose of the Lord, or the program of the Lord.

We're going to examine each of these, since they are core issues of life that control your heart and your life. If you are going to mature in Christ, you need to know the truth about each of these. Every person ever born already believes something about each of them, and if you're sitting in the Second Chair, you are believing a lie somewhere. You may try your best to be committed, but you will not succeed if there are lies anywhere.

BASIC RULE #2:

IF YOU WANT TO BE MATURE, CHANGE YOUR BELIEF ABOUT THE PERSON OF THE LORD.

One reason that Second Chair Christians do not fully commit to Christ is that they believe that Jesus is not worth their trust. Second Chair Christians secretly believe Jesus is flawed in some way, that He is not trustworthy. And don't be too quick to say this isn't true about you. I think it may be true of each of us to varying degrees at different times in our lives. I've seen the effects of distrust in the lives of many people.

I remember a time of team-building we once had at the Wilderness Training Conference, deep in the mountains of the Carolinas. More than a dozen of the organization's executives devoted a week to intense wilderness events so that we could grow close to each other. At one point, there were only four of us remaining at the bottom of a sheer cliff more than 150 feet high; the rest of the team was already cheering us. Our knees felt like jelly, and we kept asking ourselves why on the earth we had elected to do such a dumb thing as climbing a steep cliff to build teamwork! Someone on the top held the rope, while one of the men at the bottom slipped it through his safety harness. I'll never forget what happened next. The man grinned at the rest of us and yelled to the top, "I'm ready–who's holding my line? My life's in his hands."

"Vince!" came the reply.

The guy in front of me stepped back, waving his arms and shaking his head. We were all shocked when he said, "I'm not taking one step up this rock with that guy holding my rope. I don't trust him. Get me somebody else!"

The silence was deafening. I could feel the sweat roll down my face. The shock of those words left us all stunned. The utter embarrassment for the man at the top—standing in front of all his peers—was unimaginable. None of us said a word. We all sort of knew why he wouldn't put his life on the line with Vince holding the rope. But the offense of having verbalized those words threatened to negate any good that had come from our time together.

Then I heard the clicks of another man stepping in. He called out Vince's name, and stated that he had the rope. Beyond that, he didn't say a word. He simply started climbing up the face of the wall. He was willing to trust the person at the top.

And we discovered a truth that translates into who or what we trust to get us through life: a person who trusts the person at the top risks everything because he is confident that the one at the top is fully trustworthy. People who will only climb a few feet and then panic do so because they do not believe that the person who is in control of their lifelines is trustworthy.

Jesus said, "Come, follow me." And if you really trusted Him, you would take His line and follow Him up the face of any cliff. You would stop only when you decided you couldn't trust Him any further. You see, those who compromise stop somewhere on the cliff itself to say to themselves, "I just can't go any further. *I don't trust the person at the top.*"

If you want to sit in the First Chair, you'll have to learn to trust who Jesus is. You'll have to start believing that He loves you and He knows what is best. And your behavior will reveal what you really believe. Not relying on Him proves that, deep down, you don't trust Him.

BASIC RULE #3:

IF YOU WANT TO BE MATURE, CHANGE YOUR BELIEF ABOUT THE POWER OF THE LORD.

Moses threw up his hands and said, "I have had it! Enough is enough!" The people are in the wilderness, no *Food Giants* or *Safeway* stores anywhere in sight. And now they want meat. More than two million people wanted meat. So Moses got upset: "Where am I to get meat to give to all these people? For they weep all over me, saying, 'Give us meat, that we may eat'" (Numbers 11:13). The Lord heard their whining, and "the anger of the Lord was greatly aroused." He told Moses, "I will give them meat, that they may eat for a *whole month*."

That was it, the last straw for Moses. Come on, Lord, let's get serious! "Shall flocks and herds be slaughtered for them, to provide enough for them? ...Or shall all the fish of the sea be gathered together for them, to provide enough for them?" (v. 22). Everyone knows that finding meat for two million people while wandering in the desert is impossible. But notice God's response in verse 23:

> "And the Lord said to Moses, 'Has the Lord's arm been shortened? Now you shall see whether My word will befall you or not'" (Numbers 11:23).

In comparison to feeding manna to two million people every day for forty years, what was a little bit of meat? For a God who could push back the Red Sea and let the nation of Israel walk through it on dry ground, why did providing meat seem so impossible? This was the same God who had sent the plagues and flooded the world. Why should providing a little protein seem to be such an impossibility?

And what about the time He allowed Sarah to give birth at the age of ninety? The Lord had said to Abraham, "I will certainly return to you...and behold, Sarah your wife shall have a son." Sarah, who was ninety years old, was listening at the tent door. What happened next is recorded in Genesis 18:12-15: "Therefore Sarah laughed within herself, saying, 'After I have grown old, shall I have pleasure, my lord being old also?'" In other words, she laughed to herself, believing that having a baby was a total impossibility. "And then Lord said to Abraham, 'Why did Sarah laugh, saying, Shall I surely bear a child, since I am old? Is anything too hard for the Lord? At the appointed time I will return to you according to the time of life, and Sarah shall have a son.'" The Lord was asking Abraham for the reason for Sarah's unbelief. "But Sarah denied it, saying, 'I did not laugh,' for she was afraid. And He said, 'No, but you did laugh!'" The Lord knew Sarah's thoughts. When she lied, He immediately corrected her.

Just as with Moses, Sarah and Abraham did not believe God could do what He said He would do. They looked at the situation and said, "It's impossible." In both situations the Lord's response was to ask immediately why they doubted Him. To Moses He said, "Has My arm been shortened?" To Sarah, He said, "Is anything too hard for the Lord?" Both times the same crisis in belief occurred. An seemingly impossible situation led to the conclusion that even the Lord could not accomplish what He said. But both times the same answer came from the Lord: "Since when have I faced something I could not solve? Since when do I not have the power to accomplish whatever I choose?" A committed Christian believes in the power of the Lord.

What were the consequences of the unbelief? Numbers 11 tells us that the Lord indeed gave the people meat, but He sent a plague along with it because of their complaining. He accomplished what He said He would. In Sarah's case, she took matters into her own hands. She knew what God had said, for the Lord had said it over and over again. He even entered into a remarkable blood covenant with Abraham, guaranteeing the fulfillment of His promises in the most solemn way possible. Yet Sarah and Abraham did not believe God *would* keep His promise, and later that God *could* keep His promise. They both sinned with Hagar, causing problems that still plague the Jews today.

It never fails. Whenever we stop believing in God's power to do what He has promised, we compromise. We stop our commitment to God because we secretly believe that He cannot fix the particular problem we face. Second Chair people secretly believe that God is too powerless for their really big problems.

What in your life have you chosen to believe is too hard for God? Mary and Martha believed that Jesus could have healed their brother Lazarus, but after Lazarus died, they gave up on Jesus. They concluded that the Lord couldn't raise him from the dead, if they even thought of that possibility in the first place. And they certainly never thought of asking Him to do it! John records what Jesus said about not coming sooner to heal Lazarus. He purposely waited until Lazarus had been dead for four days: "And I am glad for your sakes that I was not there, that you may believe. Nevertheless let us go to him" (John 11:15).

Mary and Martha believed in the final resurrection of the dead, but they just could not believe that the Lord could raise someone from the dead while here on earth. And if even that was not too hard for Jesus, can you see the utter folly when we say to ourselves, "This is definitely too hard for God!"

We, like Mary and Martha, believe that God will raise us from the dead eventually. The Bible says it will happen, "in a moment, in the twinkling of an eye, at the last trumpet. For the trumpet will sound, and the dead will be raised incorruptible, and we shall be changed" (1 Corinthians 15:52). Can you believe in a power that big? Well, if the Lord, mighty in power and strength, is able to raise from the dead millions of people—many of whose bodies have totally disintegrated—over thousands of years of time, as well as give them brand new bodies, what is there in your life that can possibly compare to that?

Moses believed that the Lord could provide water for two million, but not that He could provide meat. Sarah believed that God could give her a son, but not through her own womb at that late age. Mary and Martha believed that the Lord could raise millions, but not one. Yet Jesus was clear and profound: "Now if God so clothes the grass of the field, which today is, and tomorrow is thrown into the oven, will He not much more clothe you, O you of little faith? Therefore do not worry, saying, 'What shall we eat?' or 'What shall we drink?' or 'What shall we wear?' For after all these things the Gentiles seek. For your heavenly Father knows that you need all these things. But seek first the kingdom of God and His righteousness, and all these things shall be added to you" (Matthew 6:30-33).

The Lord fed two million people food and water for forty years. Every day. Jesus promised He would do the same for you. He asks that your response be full commitment. He even said that, though His own words were, "Seek first the Kingdom of God and His righteousness, and all these things shall be added to you."

There is absolutely no limit to the power of the Lord.

None.

Ever.

For any person.

At any time.

If you believe that, then you will never have to look for a Hagar. You will never have to compromise again. You will wait. On the Lord. Knowing that He always keeps His promises.

BASICS RULE #4:

IF YOU WANT TO BE MATURE, CHANGE YOUR BELIEF ABOUT THE PURPOSE OF THE LORD.

Another lie that Second Chair people believe has to do with the purpose of the Lord. They don't trust the person of the Lord, they doubt the power of the Lord, and they question the purpose of the Lord. In the quiet of his heart, the Second Chair person questions the motives of the Master. You'll know the person who struggles in this area because of two reasons.

First, he has a lot of questions for the Lord, and they all begin with the word "Why?"

"Why, Lord did you...."

"Why, Lord didn't You...."

"God, how could you allow...."

"If You really were good, then You would...."

Do you know what lies beneath all those seemingly fair questions? That God has been unfair. And if you could reason with Him, then you certainly could straighten Him out. Or if you couldn't straighten Him out, you could at least prove to yourself that God isn't really good anyway. Second Chair people don't trust the heart of God to be pure. They question His purpose.

Asking "Why?" calls motive into question. People who question motive cannot be wholehearted in their support; they cannot be fully committed because they are always on guard, waiting for the Lord to let them down. Either that or they believe that the Lord is not ultimately looking out for their best.

Our enemy loves this. Even the slightest hint of this type of unbelief invites him to twist that unbelief to his great advantage and your great disaster. In fact, doubting God's motivation may be the most powerful influence in turning your heart from wanting to be a committed First Chair person. It can even make the Third Chair look enticing. If deep down inside you distrust the motivation of another person, you will be unable to interpret him without a strong negative bias. You see every action of goodness that he does for you or for others through the eyes of skepticism and doubt. Everything has a different and deeper motive behind it than the person professes. You think nothing is what it seems to be. The eyes of the heart that doubts the motivations of the Lord see Him only as the Master Manipulator, always out for his own selfish goals rather than another's best interest.

> "Now the serpent was more cunning...and said to the woman, 'You will not surely die. For God knows that in the day you eat of it your eyes will be opened, and you will be like God, knowing good and evil. So when the woman saw that the tree was....desirable to make one wise, she took it and ate of it" (Genesis 3:1, 4-6).

The same lie is there: "The Lord was withholding something from you, Eve—something wonderful! Can you believe it? Why, just look at that tree—it is 'desirable to make one wise.'" In other words, the lie is that God's real motivation is to harm you in some way. This often leads a person to conclude that if he circumvents what the Lord says, he'll be better off. The message of the serpent to Eve in the garden was this: "The Lord's command to not eat off the tree is for your harm! Disobey His command and you will be better off. Don't trust that what the Lord says really reveals the truth. Evaluate whatever command the Lord gives and make up your own mind."

That's the lie. If people believe that God's motives are not always dependable, they'd decide they'd better not take hold of the rope that's hanging from the top of a cliff. The moment that a person starts believing that God's motives are not entirely pure, he has made a choice to sit in the Second Chair. *You cannot be thoroughly committed to a person whose motives you do not trust.* You will be skeptical—especially during those times when the situation you are in seems to prove that He didn't tell you the truth about what was really going on. It is easy then to send the "why" questions screaming toward the Lord of heaven.

I remember being stuck in the Second Chair once. I mean *really* stuck. Back then I called it my "mid-life crisis." I was nearing forty and nothing was working right. The ministry wasn't satisfying. I wanted everything I didn't have. Even the proverbial "red sports car" and all that goes with it looked awfully good to this middle-aged married man. So did quitting the ministry. I didn't know what I wanted to do instead; maybe work at a bagel shop or something. Anything else...but *something* else.

Eventually, it all came to a head. I knew I had to do something, but no matter what I tried, it didn't work. So I turned to one of my mentors who had been used by the Lord numerous times during the previous twenty or so years, Dr. Howard G. Hendricks, a distinguished professor from Dallas Seminary. I called him and I told him I was stuck and that I needed help.

After only two sentences, he told me he was there for me, and that I should catch a plane the next day to go see him. He canceled some meetings and set the whole afternoon aside for me. Such friendship is a rare treasure.

When I finally sat in his office the next afternoon, I was

uncomfortable and distressed. Not because of "Prof," as we affectionately call him, but because of the internal turmoil that was raging in me. He asked me a few questions, and listened quietly. He didn't say much. I can remember sweating, just trying to explain for him as best as I could my turmoil and confusion. For as long as I live, I will never forget what he said next.

"Bruce, I can help you. Will you do what I say?"

"Well," I asked, "what do you want me to do?"

He sat quietly for a moment, and then said soberly, "Will you do what I say regardless of what I ask?"

I couldn't believe it! He wanted my commitment before telling me what it was going to be! He was keeping me purposefully in the dark!

I just sat there. Sweat dripped down my forehead. I couldn't speak. I just looked at the floor.

After a while, he said, "Bruce, do you believe I love you?"

"Yes, Prof, I know you love me."

"Then trust me."

There it was, out in the open. "Trust me." That was the problem.

For the longest time, I sat there considering his words. I knew he loved me. I knew he could be trusted. But, could I trust him this far? Could I agree to do whatever he asked, even before he told me what it was? He was asking me to trust him without an answer to the question "Why?"

After what seemed like an eternity, I finally found the words: "Yes, Prof, I know you love me–and I know that I can trust you. I will do anything you ask me to do."

He smiled with affection and gave me two different things to do. Everything in me screamed in opposition. What he was suggesting was the very opposite of what I wanted to do! I told him that I would set aside all of the emotion and arguments in my heart, and that I would do exactly what he asked me to. Then I flew home.

I did exactly what he said.

And, within three or four weeks, I was set free.

Prof's motive was his love for me. Since I could trust his motivation, I could trust his advice, even though I did not understand or agree with it. Prof had no self-interest, no selfish ambition, no hidden agenda. He had nothing, except love for me.

What is the motive of the Lord regarding you, my friend? Why is He doing the things that He is doing? When He says, "Don't eat off that tree," is it because He is withholding something good from you or seeking to harm you? If God's motive is not love for you, then what on earth is it? And what would have to happen in your life for you to start believing that God loves you? How could God prove to you that His motive is purely love for you, and nothing else, ever?

Romans 5:8 says, "In this, God proved His love for us, in that while we were yet sinners, Christ died for us."

That's profound love. God has already proved His love to us by sacrificing His only Son on our behalf. How can we entertain the thought that God is holding out on us when He has already given us the greatest gift—eternity with Him through His Son? God gave us that gift when we were still in utter and complete rebellion against Him and His Kingdom, not when we had just finished our greatest act of service for Him! Think of a long list of things you could do to prove to someone that you loved him, and rank them from easiest to the most difficult and costly. What is the most costly, most precious thing you can give for another? Is it your life? Not really. The most costly, precious thing you can give is the life of the person you love most in the universe. Would you not die for your spouse or children rather than have them die? God of heaven gave the One He loved the most in all the universe—His only Son. That is who He sent to die for His enemies. When it came to getting things right between you and Himself, God went right to the bottom of His list and made His decision. How can we ever doubt His motivation? He loves you. He has a plan and a purpose for you that demonstrates His love.

Still, it is possible to doubt His motivation, and the more you do, the more tightly you will be glued to the Second Chair and leaning toward the Third. You may believe that, if God really loved you, He'd do His best to protect you from pain and suffering. If intense or extended suffering happens to you or to the people you love, you might begin to doubt the Master's motivation. You can start to believe the lie that the absence of suffering is the proof of love.

The committed, however, know the truth and they reject that lie to the point that it is utterly repugnant to them. They destroy the lie and will not allow anything at any time to tempt them into doubting the love of God. Nothing can separate them from the love of God—not tribulation, distress, persecution—and they know that.

What about you? Do you really want to know the truth? The Bible says,

"If God is for us, who can be against us? He who did not spare His own Son, but delivered Him up for us all, how shall He not with Him also freely give us all things?

Who shall separate us from the love of Christ?

> Shall tribulation,
>
> or distress,
>
> or persecution,
>
> or famine,
>
> or nakedness,
>
> or peril,
>
> or sword?

For I am persuaded that neither death nor life, nor angels nor principalities nor powers, nor things present nor things to come, nor height nor depth, nor any other created thing, shall be able to separate us from the love of God which is in Christ Jesus our Lord."

(Romans 8:32-35, 38-39)

There is a canyon a million miles wide separating the committed from the compromisers, between the First Chair and the Second. The Second Chair person has conditions under which he will believe the Lord's love. Those conditions might be as varied as life itself, but they all fit under one of the words listed above. If the Second Chair person gets thrown in jail for standing up for Jesus, and the Lord doesn't deliver him in a "reasonable" time, he will begin to doubt the Lord's motivation is really love. He will then doubt the Lord and pull back from his commitment to Him. The First Chair person sings in prison. The love of God is with him just as much in prison as in the palace.

If the Second Chair believer becomes afflicted with some kind of disease or disability, and God doesn't deliver him, he will begin to doubt God's motivation or criticize His power. He'll pull back from his commitment. But the First Chair person says, "I will celebrate my weakness, because in it God's strength is made perfect."

If Second Chair Christians experience the intense suffering of the loss of beloved family members, their livelihood, or all their belongings, they will know for sure that the Lord is not really good–if He is, then why did He allow this to happen? They will harden their hearts and close Him out. The First Chair? Listen to another committed man, Job. He lost all of those things but he said, "Though He slay me, yet I will trust Him."

If the Second Chair believer experiences unfair treatment, pain, or abuse when he knows he is in the right, he will send out accusations toward heaven. And if "heaven" does not deliver him and bring judgment on those who are the source of the suffering, he will decide that God is unfair, unjust, and unloving. The First Chair Christian believes with complete confidence that the Lord loves him with a loyal, unending, abounding love that has no conditions and can never be stopped.

My friend, what past or present situation in your life have you decided is proof that God's motivation isn't super-abounding love for you? Before you give an answer, stand at the foot of the cross and look up, right into the heart of the Father who loves you. Every "why" will melt away with your hot tears. The only thing that dwells in the heart of the Father is love. Nothing more, nothing less. His eternal and superabundant love cries out to you. All of His love has your name on it. Everything He does is motivated by that love, regardless of what you do or say.

I've been writing about it for pages, but the truths God is calling us to believe need only those few words you probably sang as a child: "Jesus loves me, this I know, for the Bible tells me so." He loves you. He would never do anything to harm you. He only wants what is best for you. That's His purpose. If you doubt that, you will never sit in the First Chair.

1. In your own words, what is the focus of your commitment?

2. What truth do we need to know about the person of the Lord?

3. How have you seen the power of the Lord at work in your life?

4. What is the purpose of the Lord?

5. How can we change our beliefs regarding the person, power, and purpose of God?

CHAPTER SEVEN

The Secrets
of the
Committed
Part Two

As we've seen, moving to the First Chair isn't mysterious or complicated. All it takes is for you to begin to believe the truth about God. The last of what I called the "Five Secrets of the Committed" deals with something more all-consuming, and it is usually the last obstacle for the person who wants to move from the Second Chair to the First Chair. It is only after a person knows the truth about the person of the Lord, the power of the Lord, and the purpose of the Lord that he is adequately prepared to deal with the program of the Lord.

BASIC RULE #5:

IF YOU WANT TO BE MATURE, CHANGE YOUR BELIEF ABOUT THE PROGRAM OF THE LORD.

The purpose of the Lord has to do with His *motive*, while the program of the Lord has to do with His *method*. The word that questions His purpose is "*Why?*" but the question that we ask about His program is "*How?*" It is only after you believe the truth about the Lord's motive that you can fully embrace His method. His ways are not our ways, and His plans are different from ours. Sometimes we convince ourselves that we know the best method for accomplishing God's plan, but the fact is that our activities often get in the way of God's actions.

For example, everything in us rises up when His method requires us to experience pain. If *we* were in charge, our method would surely enable us to experience the absence of pain and presence of pleasure. We think that since we know the Lord, we should experience heaven in the right here and now, and we tell ourselves that if the Lord would only use that strategy of heaven with us, we would fully and immediately agree! Part of what heaven is about is the absence of all pain and suffering, the presence of pleasure (or joy) evermore. And it's easy to come to the conclusion that the Lord must have a flaw in His thinking. We admit that God's eternal strategies might be wonderful, but we think His current ones fall far short of the mark. His methods, we think, are less than the best. In fact, we might further think, they are unnecessary in accomplishing our desired results. We get to thinking that those desired results could be achieved much better, much faster by taking a different route to the desired destination. The Second Chair individual secretly believes the Lord's wisdom is flawed, and he comes up with his own plan to "help the Lord along."

Think about it. When your life is moving along wonderfully and things seem to be going just fine, how much trouble do you have with the Lord's program? None. And if you are leaning toward the First Chair, you probably find yourself actually praising Him quite a bit. But when your life develops distressing situations, and you think the pain is either too intense or seemingly without end, do you begin to have trouble with the Lord's program? The answer is always "yes" unless you are seated in the First Chair. The faith of the Second Chair person cracks under stress, but first-hand faith does not only believe the truth about the Lord's program, it fully embraces it as truth. When you sit in the First Chair, you believe in every part of the Lord's program. If you sit in the Second Chair, you believe in every part of the Lord's program except those requiring you to experience various tests and trials.

There is an undeniable link between what you believe about

the Lord's motivation and how you perceive His method. *The more you believe His motivation is love, the more you believe His method must be for your best.* The moment you doubt His method, you begin to doubt the quality of His love *and* the quality of His thinking. Doubt and belief cannot exist together. In one sense, when you doubt, you become an "unbeliever" about that thing. I think most "believers" live as "unbelievers," really.

But one of God's committed wrote a letter to some friends that is appropriate here. His friends were struggling to break free from doubts that held them in bondage to the Second Chair: he prayed "...that you may be able to comprehend...what is the width and length and depth and height–to know the love of Christ which passes knowledge!" (Ephesians 3:19). He knew that, until that issue was fully settled in their minds, they would never have faith in God's methods. The same is true for your life—if you believe His motive is grounded in love for you that nothing can change, the "Why?" question is settled and you can move into asking Him, "How, Lord?" and you will have confidence in His motives.

Are you ready to attack this extremely important issue in your life? It's possible that you don't trust the methods of God, but that simply means you don't trust His intelligence! In your opinion, how smart is He? It' easy to answer, "Oh, smarter than anyone! Ultimately smart!" But if you don't like His methods, you believe somewhere in your soul that His reasoning is flawed. Either His knowledge is limited and He doesn't know everything all of the time, or His wisdom is incomplete and His judgment is not sound. Second Chair people secretly believe that, though the Lord may know a great deal about many things, He certainly doesn't know everything all of the time. He may have great wisdom, but He does-n't know how to work things out for the best. So they ask questions like, "If God only knew that I...," or "How could God do this to me?" People of weak faith are always seeking some sort of explana-tion from God, as though the Lord needs to be accountable to them for things. A First Chair believer trusts that God's methods are sound—in all situations, for all people.

Friend, it doesn't work to *fight* the lies you believe; what you need to do is embrace the full truth of Scripture. God loves you and He is working out His perfect plan for your life. These two things go hand in hand. You cannot believe truth and a lie about the same thing at the same time. Either God is all-loving and all-wise, or He is a liar and the Bible is full of lies about Him.

Some people believe truth about the Lord in one situation, but a lie about Him in another situation. They have a wonderful faith in God regarding the things that are going great. But in the areas where things are going lousy, they have lost all hope. People who alternate between believing a lie and believing the truth are com-promisers—they are people of the Second Chair.

Movement can be in the other direction as well. What causes a Christian to move from belief to unbelief regarding the methods of the Lord? Every Christian believes in the methods of the Lord at some level, to a point. But we also get into a confidence crisis, our beliefs can begin to weaken, then to waver, and finally to crumble. "Crumbled faith" is just another name for "unfaithful." To be unfaithful means that your behavior demonstrates you have lost the faith you had in a given area. As your belief decreases, doubt increases at an equal rate. It is when faith and doubt within a person are about the same strength that the greatest struggle exists. No one can continue very long in that state of tension. When what you believe and what you doubt are almost equal in your life, you will find your emotional energy draining away, leaving you depressed and eventually forcing you to choose between one or the other. Belief or unbelief. Faith or doubt.

The average Christian's belief in the Lord's methods is chal-lenged by two things: pain and the feeling that his rights have been violated. This is because the Second Chair person has the secret thought, "The Lord will protect me from pain, and will protect my rights." When his life starts filling up with pain, he begins to doubt that God's method is good. He begins to think God doesn't really know what He's doing. Perhaps God doesn't know enough, or maybe He isn't wise enough to choose the right method. Either way reveals an unbelief in the program of the Lord.

You too will have to ask yourself some questions. Does God really love you? Does He know what He's doing? If you're not sure, you're not sitting in the First Chair. If you feel you've got to meddle with God's program to "improve" it, or if you simply reject His plan as a violation of your rights, then you've not yet learned to believe the truth about God. You're still believing a lie, and you're still in the Second Chair.

BASIC RULE #6:

IF YOU WANT TO BE MATURE, CHANGE YOUR BELIEF ABOUT THE PROVISION OF THE LORD.

This next hurdle—changing what you believe about the provision of the Lord—is often the biggest, and I'm not sure that it is ever fully realized in this life. Here's my thinking:

There comes a time in a believer's life when he no longer doubts the person of the Lord. He is utterly convinced, beyond any shadow of a doubt, that the character of the Lord is without flaw. Regardless of anything that tempts him to conclude that God is not fully good, compassionate, or loyal, the committed believer cannot and will not be moved.

There comes a season in a believer's life when he no longer doubts the power of the Lord. He is utterly convinced that God's power is without limit. Regardless of anything that tempts him to conclude that God cannot do something about a particular situation, the committed Christian cannot and will not be moved from the full assurance that the power of the Lord is never depleted.

There comes a time in a believer's life when he no longer doubts the purpose of the Lord. He is fully convinced that God's purposes are based on unconditional love and loyalty. Regardless of anything that tempts him to conclude that God has withdrawn His love, the committed Christian cannot and will not be moved from the resolute confidence that God's plan is for the best and must be altered in any way.

There comes a season in a believer's life when he no longer

doubts the program of the Lord. He is fully convinced that it is perfect in every way. He embraces the fact that the Lord alone is God, and that His plan leaves no room for improvement. Nothing tempts him to conclude that God's plan is less than perfect. He has utter confidence that the plan is for his own good and will be fully accomplished, that God's timing cannot be improved upon, and that His program always achieves His ultimate objectives. Therefore, the committed Christian is immovable regarding God's plan.

Since those four areas have such a profound impact on a person's ability to move from being a compromiser to being a person of commitment, let's review for just a moment. Believing truth in these four areas ultimately influences every other belief and behavior. There are three test areas that reveal what is in a person's heart. Each of these are talked about in Scripture, and they are usually given during times of trials.

First, you can spot a committed Christian by his words. His verbalization of what is happening in his life is full either of negatives and questions, or of positive statements of faith. He has either learned the truth and therefore does not find anything to be negative about, or he is still in process and is betrayed by his own words. Words either build up or tear down. Complaining about the circumstances ultimately opposes the Lord. A quick read through the book of Numbers will remind you how the Lord interprets the criticism of His people.

Second, you can spot a committed Christian by his actions. If his life reflects the peace of a profound inner trust, he is probably sitting in the First Chair. The fruit of the Spirit still flourishes, in the bad times as well as the good, because his fruitfulness is not related to his circumstances. Rather than drawing back during difficult times, he is enduring, looking to Jesus Christ as the source of life.

Third, you can spot a committed Christian by the trend of his life. As time passes, you see more and more of Jesus Christ reflected in his countenance, his values, and his behavior. Gentleness and love are growing. He is more concerned about serving others than in being served. His growth is evident to all who would just take a look.

But, if you want to move from the Second Chair into the First Chair, if you want to be mature in Christ, you will also need to change your belief about the provision of the Lord. Believing the truth about that underlies the life of the committed Christian. Understanding the provision of God unleashes unlimited resources that help you achieve victory in the trials that come your way, and bear fruit that lasts and glorifies God.

The first five rules enable you to remain committed to the Lord as you learn to act biblically. This next rule enables you take initiative for the Kingdom based on your commitment to Christ. The first five, then, are training for the sixth. The more skill you develop in putting the first five basics into practice, the more you will be able to achieve in this sixth area.

One way to look at the first five is as the *defensive* truths that enable you to remain committed, regardless of the length of the "race" the Lord has set before you, or its difficulty. People who have learned these basics live out the belief that:

The Lord's *character* is perfect and never changes.

The Lord's *resources* are unlimited and always available.

The Lord's *motives* can only be unconditional love and loyalty.

The Lord's *plan* is perfect, including the what, how, why, when, and where.

With the sixth basic rule of the committed, you can begin to move offensively. You start to impact the world for the cause of Christ. You learn to believe the truth about God's incredible provision for victory. People who have learned a great deal with the first five basic rules can say along with Paul, "I have learned in whatever state I am, to be content" (Philippians 4:11). But when those same people learn the sixth rule, they say, *"I can do all things through Christ who strengthens me"* (Philippians 4:13). A Christian who really believes in the provision of the Lord knows he can accomplish great things for God.

Whenever you meet a believer who lives out this truth, you see a person who is *mighty in the Spirit*. He initiates great exploits for his God while everyone else is drowning under the morass of mediocrity. Consider a few of the mighty men who demonstrate this in the Scriptures:

Jonathan—His father, King Saul, and the army of Israel cowered under the heavy hand of the powerful Philistine army camped nearby. Jonathan said to the young man who bore his armor, "Come, let us go over to the garrison of these uncircumcised; it may be that the Lord will work for us. For nothing restrains the Lord from saving by many or by few" (1 Samuel 14:6). The Lord confirmed the sign that Jonathan asked for (1 Samuel 14:7-13) and went with him. Twenty men fell before Jonathan and his armor bearer in only one acre of land. Then the Lord sent a powerful earthquake that enabled the army of Israel to defeat a far more powerful army.

Do you see Jonathan's perspective on the situation?

1. He saw the opportunity right where he was.

2. He took the initiative and went toward the situation.

3. He affirmed the Lord's leading.

4. He trusted in the strength of the Lord, not in his own strength.

5. He knew that the Lord had no difficulty defeating the enemy regardless of whether there were many with him or few.

The whole army of Israel was nearby, but no one else even thought of attacking the enemy! The situation before them looked humanly impossible. Do you know what? It always does to a Second Chair Christian. But the committed—they trust the Lord fully.

David—Turn a couple of pages in your Bible and you'll read of Jonathan's best friend, another "mighty man" even though he was still young. The whole army of Israel was camped on one side of a mountain; the Philistine army was camped on the other. In the middle was an opportunity—the impossible and threatening opportunity. A nine-foot giant named Goliath yelled each day in the valley below, "I defy the armies of Israel this day; give me a man, that we may fight together." When Saul and all of Israel heard these words, they were dismayed and "greatly afraid" (1 Samuel 17:10-11). Then David shows up at camp with some snacks for his older brothers. He sees the situation, and acts unlike every other person in the camp. *He* goes out to fight the giant! David meets Goliath with these unforgettable words:

> "You come to me with a sword, with a spear, and with a javelin. But I come to you in the name of the Lord of hosts, the God of the armies of Israel, whom you have defied. This day the Lord will deliver you into my hand... that all the earth may know there is a God in Israel. Then all this assembly shall know that the Lord does not save with sword and spear; for the battle is the Lord's, and He will give you into our hands" (1 Samuel 17:45-47).

Do you see the belief so firmly rooted in David's heart? His behavior could not help but be consistent with that truth. What was the belief and motive of this committed warrior?

"I come in the name of the Lord of hosts."
David saw himself as the servant of God.

"The Lord will deliver you into my hand—the battle is the Lord's."
David knew that the Lord's power would easily prevail.

"That the earth may know that there is a God in Israel."
David was motivated to extol and magnify the reputation of the Lord—in the eyes of the world—"for the glory of God."

Why didn't anyone else in the army take Goliath on? Because they had not become committed to the Lord enough to believe—certainly not enough to risk their lives—that He would enable them to defeat such a big obstacle. But David had. All too often, when people start to believe the truth of the Lord, they jump a mile ahead, attack a Goliath, and fail miserably. Then they want to blame the Lord for not coming through! But the Lord's arm has not weakened! Feats of might are accomplished by people of might, and becoming that takes practice. Mighty feats, both physical and spiritual, are usually accomplished by people who have trained and trained in the basics. They have become mighty in faith by living out that faith through multitudes of trials and tests that came their way.

So listen to David as he recounts the way his faith and abilities were strengthened so that he could face Goliath without fear:

> "Your servant used to keep his father's sheep, and when a lion or a bear came and took a lamb out of the flock, I went out after it and struck it, and delivered the lamb from its mouth; and when it arose against me, I caught it by its beard, and struck and killed it. Your servant has killed both lion and bear; and this uncircumcised Philistine will be like one of them, seeing he has defied the armies of the living God" (1 Samuel 17:34-36).

David had had his faith tested before. He knew God would provide for him in the face of this difficult challenge, and he trusted in that provision. David knew that Goliath would fall, and he was willing to tell everyone so as to build up their faith. Rather than cowering behind the battle line, David stepped out to fight the pagan giant, the course of his action revealing his faith.

RULE # 7:

IF YOU WANT TO BE MATURE, CHANGE YOUR BELIEF ABOUT THE TIMING OF YOUR COMMITMENT.

If you don't believe that the character of the Lord is flawed, commit yourself right now to trusting His character from here on out. Remember, He does not change!

If you don't believe that the strength of the Lord is limited, commit yourself right now to trusting His power from here on out. Remember, the God who spoke the world into existence can handle any situation that you and I can get into. I doubt if either of us will ever be in a predicament that will need anything more than a "creation of the world" miracle.

If you don't believe that the Lord is fickle or unloyal to you, commit yourself right now to trusting His love and loyalty to you from here on out. He said He would never leave you or forsake you. No matter what.

If you believe that the Lord develops an effective plan, commit yourself right now to trusting that plan from here on out. Just look at a bouquet of mixed flowers, watch an eagle soar or the sun rise over the ocean. Stop and listen to your heart beating just one of its billion times, pumping blood throughout the miles of arteries He so carefully designed. If He can figure out all those things, then perhaps He wasn't too challenged in planning out the end of things here on earth. Drop into heaven for a split second, look around, and then come on back. You'll find it's very good, and that is the place He's preparing for you. He is the same Master Planner. Give Him room—He has already planned His work. Don't even think that He won't work His plan...especially His wonderful plan for you.

Do you think the Lord would leave you helpless to work in His Kingdom? He's asked you to accomplish great exploits for Him, and He is keeping a record of everything so He can personally reward you when you meet Him face to face. Until that time, He's given you "everything you need for life and godliness," according to the Bible. Open that heavenly gift box of resources; it's for every occasion. It includes His Spirit, His spiritual gifts, His saints, His spiritual leaders, His salvation, and His Son. Use the "heavenly software" of your mind and you'll find it can process anything you face!

Now, one last question: What is stopping *you* from moving from the Second Chair of compromise to the First Chair of commitment? Only one thing has stopped anyone for the past two thousand years: lies. There are two of them. The first lie is, *"The Lord does not tell the truth and therefore I can't trust Him."* The second lie follows the first: *"Since I can't trust the Lord, I'd better not commit myself fully to Him."*

That cunning snake. He whispered a lie the first time he opened his mouth in that garden thousands of years ago. Eve knew better. So did Adam. But they doubted and stopped trusting God. As a result, they forfeited the garden. They lost the presence of the Lord. And they died.

You know that the Lord is the way. He is the truth, and He is the life. You can choose to be a person with a divided heart, or you can choose to be a person of integrity. Jesus is the Almighty King of Kings, and you can start living like He is right now. You know what the truth is. The next step is to believe it and incorporate it into your life. You can move from the Second Chair to the First Chair. You can't be mature in your spiritual life by improving your behavior. Your behavior will only change when you change the beliefs behind them.

Jesus stands at the side of the First Chair, arms outstretched. He once said, "Whosoever will may come." And He still means that. Jesus is calling *you*:

"Come to the Chair of the committed!"

STUDY QUESTIONS

1. When do you have a tendency to question the program of the Lord?

2. How can we know for certain that God knows best?

3. What are some of the ways God has proven His love for you?

4. What provision has the Lord given you for victory?

5. What will it take to make you a "mighty man of God"?

CHAPTER EIGHT

People, Possessions, or Purposelessness

The pattern of the Three Chairs affects the entire fabric of a person's life. No matter where you peel back the fabric, the differences are obvious. Whether you are a First Chair believer or a Second Chair believer, the Chair in which you sit influences your entire life. By this point, you are acquainted with a number of the differences between the Three Chairs. Now, we're going to see how the belief patterns determine how a person in each of the Three Chairs lives and what's important to him. First Chair believers are most interested in people, Second Chair believers are most interested in possessions, and Third Chair people live with a sense of purposelessness.

If you are a Second Chair believer, you may feel more convicted the more you read and think this through—this subject often hits close to home. But if you have been a First Chair believer for some time, you might almost be able to finish my sentences because you have been through this yourself. You've already experienced the competition between people, possessions, and purposelessness.

Recently, I met with a man I have been discipling for a number of years. Before he left, I loaned him a couple of books from my library that I knew would greatly stimulate his thinking about becoming more committed. The books were biographies of committed believers from previous generations. Spiritual biographies can be powerful aids: the more you read the lives of the "greats" in Christian history, the more you see the same themes repeated over and over. Christian biographies act as living parables, helping to explain the ways of God with men. Warren Wiersbe has observed that parables start off like *pictures*, something we can look at. Then, they become *mirrors*, where we can see ourselves and our lives reflected. Eventually, they become *windows*, through which we can see truth played out in all areas. It is my prayer that these next chapters will do all three of those—offer you a clear picture of the mature life in Christ, serve as a mirror for your own life, and create a window through which God can help you move toward first-hand faith.

FIRST CHAIR: PEOPLE ARE IMPORTANT

Whenever First Chair believers are nearby, their love for people is apparent. Whether they are introverts or extroverts, quiet or expressive, humorous or sober, they are always looking for ways to care for the needs of others. They invite people into their homes, get together with them elsewhere, and they reach out to be with people in many others ways as a main theme of their lives.

The early church understood this, so when they got together they shared everything in common. Christians sold their possessions to take care of one another. They gave generously to assist churches going through hard times, and they unselfishly supported Paul and other evangelists who took the Gospel to an unsaved world. Rather than thinking of their own needs, they thought of others first. And their own needs were taken care of in the process.

King David was a First Chair believer. When King Saul was after David, trying to take his life out of jealousy, David had more than one opportunity to kill him first. One time, David's men had Saul trapped in a cave. On another occasion, David sneaked into the tent where Saul lay sleeping. On neither occasion did David harm him. He knew that God had made Saul king over Israel, and he was not willing to place his own eventual right to the throne over that of another king, even though God had promised that he would be king of Israel. He befriended Saul's son, Jonathan, and after Jonathan died he took care of Mephibosheth, Jonathan's crippled son. He didn't have to do that—David did it because he cared for people. That's one of the signs of the First Chair believer.

FIRST CHAIR PEOPLE GENUINELY LOVE THOSE THE LORD LOVES

When you commit to the Lord, you become committed to what He is committed to. That is why First Chair believers love people. There is no doubt about the primary commitment of the Lord: He loves people. What was the Lord doing in the Garden of Eden but walking and talking with the first couple of His creation? He created people in His own image, so that we can have a relationship with Him unlike anything else in the universe can. Jesus even died because of the Father's genuine love for people:

"For God so loved the world that He gave His only begotten Son, that whoever believes in Him should not perish but have everlasting life. For God did not send His Son into the world to condemn the world, but that the world through Him might be saved" (John 3:16-17).

Flash forward to the end of the story, the Book of Revelation, and you can see the Lord's heart revealed in the last few chapters. You see people everywhere, and God choosing to be right in with them:

"And I heard a loud voice from heaven saying, 'Behold, the tabernacle of God is with men, and He will dwell with them, and they shall be His people, and God Himself will be with them and be their God'" (Revelation 20:3).

When Jesus spoke of His purpose on earth, He said, "For even the Son of Man did not come to be served, but to serve, and to give

His life a ransom for many" (Mark 10:45). Jesus always had time for people, no matter who came to Him. Wherever you turn in the four Gospels, you cannot escape the fact that the Lord's love has always been for people. He hasn't changed, from the Garden of Eden to this very moment, and He won't change once time has ended and there is a new heaven and new earth. The Lord's highest priority will always be people, and He genuinely loves people of all races in all situations. We teach our children that basic truth about the love of God when we have them sing, "Jesus loves the little children, all the children of the world; red and yellow, black and white, they are precious in His sight. Jesus loves the little children of the world."

Therefore, if you embrace the Lord in total commitment, you will embrace His love for others. This primary characteristic of loving people grows naturally out of your commitment to Him; the pattern of your commitment to the Lord precedes your love and service to His people.

Paul didn't mince any words about the importance of love for people when he wrote what are perhaps the most well-known words of love in the history of the world:

> "Though I speak with the tongues of men and
> of angels, *but have not love,*
> I have become as sounding brass or a clanging cymbal.
> And though I have the gift of prophecy
> and understand all mysteries and all knowledge,
> and though I have all faith, so that I could remove mountains,
> but have not love, I am nothing.
> And though I bestow all my goods to feed the poor,
> and through I give my body to be burned,
> but have not love, it profits me nothing."
>
> (1 Corinthians 13:1-3)

Love for people flows from the heart of a person committed to the Lord: "And above all things have fervent love for one another..." (1 Peter 4:8a).

FIRST CHAIR PEOPLE HUMBLY SERVE
THOSE THE LORD SERVES

Peter had just ruined his life. He had denied the One he loved and served, betraying Christ through his words and actions. Peter knew it was all over. What he didn't know was that Jesus defined "all over" much differently from how he did. After He rose from the dead, the Lord appeared to His eleven disciples. He asked Peter, "Simon, son of Jonah, do you love Me more than these?" Jesus was referring to the very best friends Peter had in the world, his fellow disciples. What Jesus wanted to know was, "Do you love me *more than* you love others?" He was once again raising the issue of complete commitment, even in the midst of Peter's worst failure. Could the Lord still be Number One, even to "such a sinner" as Peter? The answer is a resounding "Yes!" Commitment to Christ does not make a person sinless (though, as it has been said, it may make you *sin less!*).

What happened next was amazing. Jesus forged an unexpected link. Peter affirmed that the Lord was first in his life by saying, "Yes, Lord; You know that I love You," and Jesus said, "Feed my lambs." The Lord connected Peter's love for Him with serving the needs of His people. That same emphasis is present for all First Chair believers. It cannot be otherwise. People are the heartbeat of the Lord, and the hearts of those whose hearts beat in sync with His must also beat for people.

Listen to the heart of this First Chair believer:

"You know, from the first day that I came to Asia, in what manner I always lived among you, serving the Lord with all humility, with many tears and trials which happened to me by the plotting of the Jews; and how I kept back nothing that was helpful, but proclaimed it to you, and taught you publicly and from house to house, testifying to Jews, and also to Greeks, repentance toward God and faith toward our Lord Jesus Christ" (Acts 20:18b-21).

Paul loved people. He once sent another First Chair believer named Timothy to serve a group of people because he couldn't do it himself. In sending his young friend, Paul said, "For I have no one like-minded, *who will sincerely care for your state. For all seek their own, not the things which are of Christ Jesus*" (Philippians 2:20-21). There is, throughout Scripture, a powerful link between loving God and loving people. First Chair people do not seek having their own needs met first; instead, they think of the needs of others. His own personal needs get relocated to third priority: Jesus first, others second, you last. And your needs will be met by another person as well.

Listen to how Paul described yet another First Chair person: "I considered it necessary to send to you Ephaphroditus, my brother...since he was longing for you all...hold such men in esteem, because for the work of Christ, he came close to death, *not regarding his life, to supply what was lacking in your service*" (Philippians 2:25ff). That "work of Christ" that Ephaphroditus came close to death to accomplish was meeting the needs of a group of people. That sounds just like Jesus, doesn't it?

This kind of love and service characterizes those who are thoroughly committed to Jesus Christ. When those first few believers got together, they treated one another as Jesus had treated people. Just read through a few verses that describe those First Century committed to see how they lived and loved:

"Now all who believed were together,
and had all things in common,
and sold their possessions and goods, and divided them among all,
as anyone had need.
So continuing daily with one accord in the temple,
and breaking bread from house to house,
they ate their food with gladness and simplicity of heart,
praising God and
having favor with all the people.
And the Lord added to the church daily those
who were being saved."

(Acts 2:44-47)

The fact that they loved one another so deeply was like a fragrant aroma, drawing others into the family of love. Their willingness to humbly serve one another brought them favor with outsiders who could then be introduced to the God of love.

FIRST CHAIR PEOPLE PRAY FOR THOSE WHOM THE LORD PRAYS FOR

When the Lord told Abraham, in Genesis 18:20, that "the outcry against Sodom and Gomorrah is great, and because their sin is very grievous" He was going to destroy those cities, what did Abraham do? He interceded with intense and fervent pleading on behalf of those rebellious people, "for their sakes." Abraham loved people, so he prayed to God for them.

When Israel rebelled against God at Kadesh Barnea, the place where they fully rejected His gift of the Promised Land, the Lord told Moses that He was going to "strike Israel...and disinherit them...and make of (Moses) a nation greater and mightier than they" (Numbers 14:11). Moses interceded with fervent and intense prayer on behalf of the very people who had wanted to stone him earlier. Moses loved people, so he prayed for them.

When you read the Epistles, you cannot miss the depth and consistency of Paul's prayers for people—over and over again. He loved people, so he prayed continually for them. This is, I think, one of the most astounding verses in the entire Bible:

"I tell you the truth in Christ, I am not lying, my conscience also bearing me witness in the Holy Spirit, that I have great sorrow and continual grief in my heart. *For I could wish that I myself were accursed from Christ for my brethren*, my kinsmen according to the flesh..." (Romans 9:1-3).

Paul loved his people so completely, so deeply, so passionately that he was willing even to be "accursed from Christ" for the sake

131

of their salvation. How deep that love is!

Another of the early Christians, a kindred spirit with Paul, insisted on telling the truth to his fellow Jews in need of salvation, no matter what the cost. Paul was there, before he met the Lord on the road to Damascus:

> "And they stoned Stephen as he was calling on God and saying, 'Lord Jesus, receive my spirit.' Then he knelt down and cried out with a loud voice, 'Lord, do not charge them with this sin.' And when he had said this, he fell asleep" (Acts 7:59-8:1a).

Stephen loved people so much that he could pray for their forgiveness *even as they were putting him to death*. Love people and pray for them. Those are the marks of a First Chair person.

Naturally, the more you love, the more you serve the person or people you love. The more wholly you serve, the more you pray. The more you pray, the more impact you have in the lives of those you pray for.

Take a moment for a little self-examination, and mark the chart below.

Point of Evaluation	Not often	Sometimes	Usually	Fervently
"I love people"				
"I serve people"				
"I pray for people"				
My summary thought about my progress:				

SECOND CHAIR: POSSESSIONS ARE IMPORTANT

The majority of believers sit in the Chair of compromise, making other people take a back seat. They do not love, serve or pray for others on a regular basis. Something else always takes priority, and that "something" soon determines everything in that person's life. If you scored strongly in the above self-evaluation, as you read this section you will probably experience moments of affirmation about some of the hard decisions you have made because of your commitment to the Lord. If, on the other hand, you didn't do so well above, you might come face to face with some giants that still wander the mountains and valleys of your life. Giants are powerful and painful to deal with, but they can be defeated through commitment. It is possible for you to find liberty, freedom, fulfillment, and joy, but it will not be easy.

If a believer's life is not filled with love for others, service to others, and prayers for others, what is it filled with? Each of us pursues what we consciously or subconsciously find appealing because life must be full of something. The more appealing something is to us, the more passionate and focused we are about it, and the more we dedicate our thoughts, our time, and our energy to attaining it.

There are many options for the person who doesn't choose to pursue and serve the Lord and His people, but nearly anything else you choose to fill your life with fits one of these four categories:

1. Desire to acquire possessions—getting or saving great amounts.
2. Desire for personal pleasure—enjoying leisure or sensuality.
3. Desire for power and prestige—controlling and being in charge.
4. Desire to serve people—serving the needs of others.

Think about everyone you know—your family, close friends, people at church and work, sports teammates, neighbors, and others with whom you come in contact. What percentage of them would you put into each of these four categories? Turn on your television and watch the advertisements. What values are promoted there most often? You see, everybody fits into one of those four categories.

The Four Main Desires of People				
Category	Category #1	Category #2	Category #3	Category #4
Personal Desire	Desire to Acquire *Possessions*	Desire for Personal *Pleasure*	Desire for *Power* and Prestige	Desire to Serve *People*
Percentage of my friends and family Percentage as portrayed in the media				

Now, what really motivates you? Take a look back through your calendar of activities, or think back through your week. What were you trying to achieve? What did you dream about? What would your friends say about you? What are you giving your life to achieve? In the chart below, put a 1 in the category that best repre-

The Four Main Desires in My Life as Reflected in my thoughts and those who know me				
Category	Category #1	Category #2	Category #3	Category #4
Personal Desire	Desire to Acquire *Possessions*	Desire for Personal *Pleasure*	Desire for *Power* and Prestige	Desire to Serve *People*
My life currently reflects this				

sents you, a 2 in the next best category, a 3 in the next, and a 4 in the category that represents you the least.

How do these fit into the principle of the Three Chairs? They are behaviors that reflect your beliefs. They reveal the Chair in which you sit. For example, consider the life of King David. He was a person after the Lord's own heart. Everywhere you look in the Bible, you find him thinking, even seeking, to serve others. Then, when his son Solomon became king, he followed in the same footsteps. The Lord appeared to him in a dream to say, "Ask! What shall I give you?" and Solomon's First Chair values are evident in his reply: "Therefore give to Your servant an understanding heart to judge Your people, that I may discern between good and evil. For who is able to judge this great people of yours?" Solomon's request pleased the Lord, so God said, "Because you have asked this thing, and have not asked long life for yourself, nor have asked riches for yourself, nor have asked the life of your enemies, but have asked for yourself understanding to discern justice, behold, I have done according to your words...and I have also given you what you have not asked: both riches and honor" (1 Kings 3:9, 11-13). Solomon loved the Lord, and he walked in his father's footsteps as he served God.

Imagine it. Your father is King David, whose heart for God is legendary. In response to your request, the Lord gives you more wisdom and judgment than any other person in history. How would you live your life? How would you do in the most important things of life? This is how Solomon did it:

"For it was so, when Solomon was old, that ...*his heart was not loyal to the Lord* his God, as was the heart of his father David. For Solomon went after Ashtoreth the goddess of the Sidonians, and after Milcom the abomination of the Ammonites. Solomon did evil in the sight of the Lord, and did not fully follow the Lord, as did his father David. Then Solomon built a high place for Chemosh the abomination of Moab...and for Molech the abomination of the people of Ammon...so the Lord became angry with Solomon, *because his heart had turned from the Lord God of Israel...*" (1 Kings 11:4-9).

What drew Solomon's heart away from its place in the First Chair so that he ended his life sitting in the Second Chair and leaning as far as he could toward the Third? I'm convinced that *possessions* became a controlling factor for him. They became too important. Possessions are what is important to all who sit in the Second Chair. David's charge to Solomon in 1 Kings 2:2-3, right before his death, was:

"I go the way of all the earth; be strong, therefore, and prove yourself a man. And *keep* the charge of the Lord your God: To walk in His ways, to *keep* His statutes, His commandments, His judgments, and His testimonies, *as it is written in the Law of Moses,* that you *may prosper* in all that you do and wherever you turn."

The Law of Moses contains many specific directions for the kings of Israel, but Deuteronomy 17:14-20 stands out above all the rest. The kings of Israel are not to do three specific things. First, the king "shall not *multiply horses* for himself, nor cause the people to return to Egypt to multiply horses, for the Lord has said to you, 'You shall not return that way again.'" So the king should not be stockpiling a bunch of horses, nor sending his people to Egypt to get them. Second, "Neither shall he *multiply wives* for himself, lest his heart turn away." The king of Israel was not to have more than one wife. Third, "Nor shall he greatly *multiply silver and gold* for himself." So the king should not be greedy, storing up a pile of earthly wealth. Those things will turn his heart from God.

Take a look at what Solomon did with his life, though. First Kings 4:26 reads, "Solomon had forty thousand stalls of horses for his chariots, and twelve thousand horsemen." In chapter ten we also read the words, "And Solomon had horses imported from Egypt...and exported them to all the kings of the Hittites and the kings of Syria."

Solomon sinned by importing the very things (horses) God told him not to from the very place God told him not to (Egypt). He then complicated the sin by selling them to his nation's enemies. It wasn't that God didn't like horses; He didn't want the king to put building a vast army ahead of Himself. Was Solomon compelled to do this because he was just a horse-lover? Probably not, or God would not have been so upset. The problem was that Solomon set out to get the things God promised him his own way.

Solomon was also given explicit instructions to not multiply wives. But 1 Kings reveals that "King Solomon loved many foreign women, as well as the daughter of Pharaoh: women of the Moabites, Ammonites, Edomites, Sidonians, and Hittites–from the nations of whom the Lord had said to the children of Israel, 'You shall not intermarry with them, nor they with you. For surely they will turn away your hearts after their gods.' Solomon *clung* to these in love." The Bible records that he had seven hundred wives and three hundred concubines, "and his wives turned away his heart from God."

Solomon sinned by marrying women from the nations Israel was commanded to destroy. Then, he complicated that sin by worshipping the gods of his foreign wives, and by building temples and high places so his wives could worship their idols. Solomon also sinned by enticing the entire nation of Israel to follow his example of idolatrous worship—where the leader goes, the people follow. He forsook the Lord for the gods of his enemies. Again, what motive did God have for giving clear instruction about wives, and what motive did Solomon have for disobeying the Lord? Did Solomon have three hundred wives because he thought it was the right thing to do, or because he was seeking pleasure?

Before you offer an answer, note that Solomon was also warned not to multiply silver and gold. Second Chronicles 9:13 records that "the weight of gold that came to Solomon yearly was six hundred and sixty-six talents of gold." That would be almost $4 billion by today's standards. What do you think was behind God's clear instructions about wealth, and what *desire* in Solomon was driving him to hoard possessions?

THE ALL IMPORTANT WORDS

I think we can understand Solomon's actions better by reading again the three things the Lord commanded His kings never to do. Look at the repeated two-word phrase:

"But he shall not multiply horses *for himself*...."

"Neither shall he multiply wives *for himself*, lest his heart turn away...."

"Nor shall he greatly multiply silver and gold *for himself*...."

The problem was that he was doing these things "for himself." When you desire those things for yourself, you fall into the trap that is woven into the pattern of the Second Chair. Rather than focusing on God, your focus shifts to yourself. Rather than focusing on loving others, your focus shifts to loving yourself. The danger to your spiritual life is that you'll eventually become much more concerned with yourself than you are with God.

John understood this. He talked very clearly about how the "self" desires three things:

"Do not *love* the world or the things in the world. If anyone *loves* the world, the *love* of the Father is not in him. For all that is in the world —

the lust of the *flesh*,

the lust of the *eyes*,

the *pride of life* —

is not of the Father but is of the world" (1 John 2:15-16).

The pivotal word is "love." What you love is revealed by the choices you make. Either you love the world and the things of the world, or you love the Father and the things of the Father. John describes the three main desires that all men and women deal with while on this earth: power, pleasure, and possessions. How do those relate to horses, wives, and wealth, do you think? These same three issues have been tempting us since the Garden of Eden. The serpent offered wisdom, tasty food, and a pleasing looking fruit—power, pleasure, and possessions—and we all want them. Everyone throughout history has wanted them. They were even the same sources of temptation that Satan threw at Jesus when He was in the wilderness. The devil offered Christ food—bread after such a long fast. He offered Christ wealth—the possessions of the kingdoms of the world. He offered Christ power—the kingdom of this world without the pain of the cross. But to do so, Christ would have to disobey the Father. So the Lord said "no," because He loved His Father and he knew that the love of the Father is in direct opposition to the love of this world. Do you see how John categorizes the longings of this world for us?

The Desire	Pleasure	Possession	Power/Prestige
1 John 2	Lust of the flesh	Lust of the eyes	Pride of life
Deuteronomy 17	Don't multiply wives	Don't multiply wealth	Don't multiply horses
Genesis 3	"good for food"	"pleasant for the eyes"	"desirable to make one wise"
Matthew 4	"make stones become bread"	"give the kingdoms and their glory"	"throw yourself down"

Behind all of these is love. What do you love? Solomon had been told not to love other things, not to "multiply *for yourself*," but he disobeyed because he loved the things of this world. At some time in the life of every believer, the Lord begins to put on the pressure to see if you'll choose Him above everything else. Friend, *if you don't choose the Lord, you will choose something else.* When you choose something else, you automatically do not choose the Lord. Ultimately, any other choice you make will be for pleasure, possessions, power, or a combination of them. Your choice will seem normal. It will even seem logical. But, those choices will lead to further choices, all going in the wrong direction. The pull of the world and the things of the world is unrelenting, and the person who sits in the Second Chair does not have the commitment he needs to resist, just as it was for the wisest man who ever lived.

The Bible tells us that Solomon's *"heart was not loyal to the Lord His God"* (1 Kings 11:4b). His heart became compromised. His heart became divided. Then his heart became disloyal. Ultimately his heart became filled with idolatry because he chose to love the world and the things of the world more than God. When you do that, the love of the Father is not in you.

Jesus said the same thing in even more pointed words: "No one can serve two masters; for either he will *hate* the one and *love* the other, or else he will be *loyal* to the one and *despise* the other. You cannot serve God and mammon" (Matthew 6:24). Those are convincing words. You cannot be loyal to both. Loving God and loving money are mutually exclusive, and you will serve one or the other.

I appreciate the strength with which Jesus spoke. John talked of *loving* the world, and said that if we *love* the world we won't *love* God. Jesus puts it in even stronger terms. You either *love* God and *hate* money, or you *love* money and *hate* God. There's no middle ground. Your choice will ultimately determine whom you serve. Your choice will determine your master. Your choice will determine everything in your life.

Up to this point in your life, what has been your choice? Take a look at your checkbook. Who have you invested your time and treasure serving? Jesus said, "Where your heart is, there will your treasure be also."

THE FOCUS OF THE THIRD CHAIR:
PURPOSELESSNESS

When you grow up in a Second Chair home, one that knows the Lord but chooses the ways of the world in its values and desires, you grow up on very unstable and unsteady ground. You hear your parents talk about valuing one thing but you see them living in a way that values another. The Lord is viewed as important and as the Savior, but they are not loyal to him and His Kingdom. You vicariously experience the emptiness of their pursuits. You know first-hand not of their faith but of their failure. The "rat-race" never ends for them, and "more" is always the focus of their appetites but "more" never satisfies. Everything has to be bigger. Everything has to get better. Larger. Higher. Greater. The pursuit of possessions in your parents is like trying to fill an endless black hole. The joke about "keeping up with the Jones's" soon becomes a curse. No matter what your parents go after, they never seem to be satisfied. No matter what they stuff into their lives next, seeking lasting peace and enduring fulfillment, it doesn't work. The more that's crammed in, the emptier it seems.

That craving for possessions is the "master" that your parents serve. And you vow to never live your life like they did. Possessions didn't work. Having more and more things didn't bring happiness, so you reject materialism as god. But, at the same time, you have seen that the other "master" your parents claimed to follow, Jesus Christ, didn't work for them either. Religion and church didn't do much for your parents except make them get out of bed on Sunday morning, when they really wanted to be sleeping in or playing golf. You decided after years of being forced to attend church that it doesn't seem to work for most people. So, you vow, one Sunday morning after pleading with your parents not to make you go to church, that you won't live your life like they did. No materialism, and no religion. No focus on possessions, and no focus on the Lord.

To be honest with you, both decisions make sense to me, at least on the surface. There is one flaw, however: you only have two choices—serving the world or serving God. If you reject both, you will never discover the third option. The problem is that most

Christians try and do both. They try to stay in the middle, getting a little bit of God and a lot of the world. But Christ said you can't do that. You may be looking for another purpose, but you'll never find it. Instead, you'll struggle with a deep sense of purposelessness, never being able to make sense out of life.

That's the pattern of someone in the Third Chair—purposelessness. He is seeking a better way, another alternative, but there *are* no other alternatives. You either embrace God's way or you embrace Satan's world. You either commit yourself to God's values or you commit yourself to fulfilling your own selfish desires.

Many people in the Third Chair become loners. Some become ruthless. Many turn to violence, or wander in immorality and escapism. If there is no purpose to life, why go on living? The person on the Third Chair will discover, like the writer of Ecclesiastes, that everything they want to achieve is empty and filled with vanity. Purposelessness becomes their distinguishing mark.

You know, you are right: the things a person in the Second Chair seeks never ultimately satisfy anyone. "Things," "good times," and money cannot fill the void in a person's heart anymore than "religion," "church," and "good values" can. But there is another way.

The Lord Jesus said it this way: "I am the way."

Do you doubt Him? He also said, "I am the truth."

What about life—do you seek life, *real* life? Jesus also said, "I am the life."

If you're in the Third Chair, it may be time for you to stop looking back and blaming. It may be time for you to start looking up and believing. Jesus calls you to experience life and truth. He loves you, and He died to set you free from the Third Chair. He has a First Chair with your name on it.

Come to Him. You'll find Him the quickest when you get on your knees. Tell Him your need and your belief in His death on the cross to pay for your sins. Ask Him for His gift of salvation. He's ready to give it to you. His arms have been open for you a long time. Go fill them with yourself.

The Lord wants your undivided heart. He wants you to be committed to Him. There is purpose in this life, but it's only found in Him. You won't find it in power, or pleasure, or possessions. You'll only find it in Jesus. He wants your complete loyalty. He wants your complete trust. He wants you.

1. How do you see people pursuing pleasure, power, and possessions in our culture?

2. In what ways do "possessions" become the focus of the Second Chair person?

3. In your own words, why do third generation people often reject the values of their parents and become Third Chair people?

4. How can a Christian develop a love for people?

5. How would you evaluate your own life in terms of hating the world and loving God?

CHAPTER NINE

From Possessions to People

Think of your life as a line. A line, according to my high school geometry teacher, begins with a dot, then goes out into space. It never ends, but continues forever. You could fly on a supersonic jet for the rest of your life and you'd never come to the end of that line. Now compare that line with the dot that started it. They might seem to be the same thing when you begin drawing, but once you see in your mind's eye that line going on forever, you get a better sense of how different they are.

Your life started at one particular spot, just like that dot. But it will continue forever, like the line. No matter what happens, your life will never cease to exist. Our time on earth might seem long, but in the big picture of eternity our entire lives take place at that one dot. Eternity is the long, endless line. Ten thousand years won't even be the opening day of eternity. In fact, we won't even have "years" in the afterlife, because there is no time in eternity.

Each of us will spend all of eternity doing one of two things: we will either enjoy God's presence or curse His justice. You see, the Bible is clear that what we do in this short part of our lives here on earth determines everything about the long part of our lives in eternity. What you do with your "dot" determines the course of your "line."

In business, we call this principle "leverage"–the ability to control a lot with a little. The greater amount you can control with the same effort, the greater leverage. In real estate, the smaller the down payment on a piece of property you purchase, the more leverage you have. That is, with only a small amount of money you are controlling a large amount of money, represented by the house. If your $100,000 house went up by five percent in one year, your investment would have earned $5,000. If you had invested $20,000 as a down payment you would have earned twenty-five percent interest on your money. If, however, you had only invested $5,000 down, then you would have earned one hundred percent interest.

"Leverage" is also at work in our lives when it comes to where you will be in eternity. With the investment of less than one hundred years, you control your destiny of more than one hundred billion years. With an investment of less than one hundred years, you control what will happen to you for a period that cannot be measured, that goes on forever. Whenever I am faced with an important decision, I practice what I call the "Future Perfect Principle." I put the issue into clearer focus by enlarging the context. I ask myself, "Ten years from now, what will have been the correct decision? How will I evaluate my decision then?"

Recently, I was discussing options for college with an outstanding high school student. At the beginning of the conversation she was leaning against one particular college, even though it had arguably the best training for her chosen field. She didn't want to attend that school because it had some rather unique requirements that frustrated her. She was focused only on those frustrations, even though the program was the best in the country. We pretended that we were talking ten years from now, when she would be nearing thirty. I asked how she would evaluate those frustrations from that perspective. She immediately saw my point—those issues wouldn't even *be* issues when she is that age. She laughed, and agreed to reconsider her decision.

You see, that young lady's decision not to go to the best institution because of a couple of minor irritations was short-sighted. She was focusing on the wrong issues to make a decision that would affect her for the rest of her life. There is a profound truth here, my friend. When you compare these few years of your life to the whole thing, you will look at the irritations, the challenges, and the sacrifices in an entirely different way. We all seem to focus on the present. We live for the moment, expect instant everything, and can think only of the immediate need. We need to develop the habit of thinking for the future.

Many books are written each year offering somebody's ideas about how to best live your life, but most of them are simply untried principles or flabby philosophy. The Bible offers the rock solid truth of God. When you need wisdom about how to live your life, crack open your Bible and start reading. Don't accept the notion that "the Bible has many interpretations." *People* have many interpretations, but God has only one interpretation in mind. So when you look at the truths of Scripture, take time and figure out exactly what the Bible is teaching before you try to put it into practice. Before founding Walk Thru the Bible Ministries, I taught at Multnomah School of the Bible in Portland, Oregon. One of my privileges was teaching "How to Study the Bible" on four different levels: to freshmen, juniors, seniors, and graduate students. Every semester, we would start out with these principles: 1) read the Bible for yourself to see what it says, 2) interpret what you think it meant to the original author and recipients, and finally 3) take practical steps in *doing* what it teaches. Observation first, interpretation second, application third. When we jump to application before we know what the Bible says, we usually encounter unnecessary difficulties.

The purpose of this chapter is to find out more about what the Bible teaches in regard to hindrances to becoming a First Chair believer. Since the obstacles involved are strongholds of untruth, the only way to tear them down is to study the truth of the Bible.

THE TRANSFORMATION FROM
POSSESSIONS TO PEOPLE

As we have already seen, Jesus summarized the issue clearly: "No one can serve two masters; for either he will hate the one and love the other, or else he will be loyal to the one and despise the other. You cannot serve both God and money" (Matthew 5:24). Christ forever polarized the issue into two camps, and you have to be in one or the other. The Lord didn't leave any room to wriggle out of this by saying, "That does not apply to me." This idea is universal and unbreakable.

We can see a couple of things about money and possessions in just this one verse:

1. There are two masters—one is God and the other is money.

2. No one can serve both—one reigns and the other doesn't.

3. Because God and money are masters, people serve them.

4. Everyone serves one or the other.

5. The choice of which to serve is up to the person.

6. Jesus does not tell us what "mammon" (Aramaic for *riches*) is except to say that it is a master and that people who don't serve God serve it.

7. Twice Christ describes contrasts by the words "either" and "or else."

8. The first contrast is one of *emotion*, the second is one of *allegiance*.

Two emotions occur in a person, regardless of whether he serves God or money. Those emotions are the exact opposite of each other. One is the extreme positive and desirable emotion, "love," while the other is the extreme negative and undesirable emotion, "hate." There is no middle ground. You may feel the struggle of the choice, but you cannot love both. If a person loves God then he hates money; if he loves money, he hates God. Jesus says it is impossible to love God and money at the same time, that they are in direct competition.

The other contrast Jesus makes is one of *allegiance, respect, and honor.* You will give your allegiance either to God or you will offer it to money. To be loyal to one is to despise the other. Why would the Lord make *this* such an adversarial issue? I'm not aware of any other time when Christ offers such a blatant choice. We could understand it better if He had said, "Everyone either follows God or Satan." But money? The Bible talks more about "money" than it does about prayer. It has more to say about "money" than marriage, the family, or even the person and work of the Holy Spirit. Since God sees it as an important issue, we'd better understand it.

Watch any television show and what do you see during the commercials? Pick up any magazine and what do you see between articles? Drive down nearly any highway in the nation and what do you see on the billboards alongside? Listen to any radio station for more than a few moments and what will you hear? It's undeniable and universal: everything relates to earning and spending money. Earn more and you can spend more. That's the pattern of our society. Even on the leading Christian college campuses, when I ask students why they are majoring in a given field, the response is always the same: "That's where the money is." This is not new in the 90's—it has been the typical response over the past 20 years.

When Jesus said, "No one can serve two masters," He used two interesting Greek words. For "master" He used the word *kurios*, which literally means "Lord." The word implies being supreme. You choose either God or possessions to be the lord of your life. For "serve" He uses the Greek word *douleo*, which means to be in bondage to. The one who is your lord has you as his slave. When college students say they are selecting a major because of the money they can earn from it, they are planning to let money rule supreme. They have, to one degree or another, already become slaves to cash. There's obviously nothing wrong with having a job or earning money. The Scriptures are very clear that we are to work so that we can eat and provide for those in need. But to put ourselves in bondage to such a temporal lord as money during the few years we have on this earth seems the height of folly.

Every once in a while, I'll hear something very different from a student. Sometimes, they will say, "I chose this because I think it's the best way to use my gifts and talents to serve the Lord most effectively." Sound unique? It is, and it's as rare as First Chair believers themselves. Second Chair Christians serve mammon and First Chair believers serve God. The reason the Bible speaks so frequently and so forcefully about money is because there are so many people sitting in the Second Chair.

As I walked with my wife across the courtyard of a large hotel in San Diego years ago, a pastor warmly called out our names. We were all there for a national conference and I was one of the plenary speakers. I had an exchange with that pastor that I will never forget. He invited me to come and speak at his large and prestigious church. I thanked him for the honor of the request, but unfortunately I already had a full calendar. I added that if he would be kind enough to send me a letter, I would consider it for the future.

When he realized that it didn't look good to get me booked in his church, he said, "We'll give you a generous honorarium!" I simply nodded and smiled, hoping he'd further get the point that I was not available.

"No, really," he said. "We want you to come—we'll even fly you and your wife out, and give you a very generous check!"

"Just send me a letter," I said.

"Why, we'll even send you both to Hawaii for a week, all expenses paid."

I just looked at him. I didn't really know what to say, except what I was thinking: "Pastor, I thank you for your kind and generous invitation—but it grieves me to see that you think I am motivated to minister because of the money you will pay me. I never ask what the honorarium will be, and I never request one. Ministry is not to be motivated by money."

I never spoke at his church, and I'm sorry to say that he's out of the ministry now—got caught up in a real estate venture that nearly destroyed him.

I cannot serve God and money. As soon as I start serving money I have stopped serving God. I struggled with what Jesus said for years, and I'm embarrassed by the reason: I simply didn't believe it could be true. But it is. Whenever I start to strongly desire money, or the things that money can buy, I am in serious danger. Do you know what word Webster's dictionary defines as "to strongly desire"? *Covet.* The Apostle Paul had this to say about that in Colossians 3:5:

"Therefore put to death your members which are the on the earth: fornication, uncleanness, passion, evil desire, and *covetousness, which is idolatry.*"

That's it! Covetousness is idolatry! No wonder Christ said it's either God or money. Money is an idol. Unlike any other country in the world today, the United States is rampant with the idolatry of money. Money rules, not God. People serve money, not God.

Ask yourself what you exchanged your life for this week. What did you seek to achieve by the end of the week? What did you do with your time? What did you do with your talents? What did you do with your treasure? In some ways, each of us is the sum of how he has spent his time, talents, and treasure—you are, and I am. Once you have taken out your time, talents, and treasure, there's not much left to your life! So what's a person to do?

Jesus didn't leave us without an answer:

"Therefore do not worry, saying, 'What shall we eat?' or 'What shall we drink?' or 'What shall we wear?' For after all these things the Gentiles seek. For your heavenly Father knows that you need all these things. But seek first the kingdom of God and His righteousness, and all these things shall be added to you" (Matthew 6:31-33).

Put very simply, Jesus says, "Don't worry about it. God will take care of you." The same One who knows all of your needs will provide. Your needs may be very different from your wants, however. So rather than seeking all the things that the pagans are seeking, seek the Lord. In the same way that pagans seek money, a follower of Jesus must seek God's Kingdom. We can't do both, so we have to choose what we'll spend our time and energy on.

Second Chair believers are more interested in pursuing money and attending church only on the weekends. First Chair believers seek the Kingdom of the Lord and His righteousness all the week long. If you choose to sit in the First Chair with them, you will have to serve Him and not money. You will have to love Him and hate money. You will have to be loyal to Him and despise money.

Remember the Apostle John's words: "Do not love the world or the things in the world. If anyone loves the world, the love of the Father is not in him." *Money is the main thing in this world.* The world runs on money. The things of this world are purchased with money. John's words could be paraphrased, "Don't love money. If anyone loves money, the love of God is not in him." As we've already seen, to love money is to worship an idol. That's why Paul warns believers,

> "But *those who desire to be rich* fall into temptation and a snare, and into many foolish and harmful lusts, which drown men in destruction and perdition. For the love of money is a root of all kinds of evil, for which some have strayed from the faith in their greediness, and pierced themselves through with many sorrows. But you, O man of God, flee these things, and pursue righteousness, godliness, love, patience, gentleness..." (1 Timothy 6:9-11).

Paul tells us what the dangerous and painful consequences are in the present for those who worship the idol of money. Their desire to be rich will destroy them. Set up as a chart, Paul's instruction looks this way:

The One Requirement:	The Four Dangers:	The Two Results:
"Those who desire—"	*"They fall into—"*	*"Which drown men in—"*
"To be Rich"	1. "Temptation"	1. "Destruction"
	2. "Snare"	2. "Perdition"
	3. "Many foolish lusts"	
	4. "Many harmful lusts"	

Loving money is not something that will get you in trouble "someday." There are very real and present consequences for those whose primary desire is to be rich. There are extra and unnecessary temptations, snares that can trap you, foolish lusts that waste our hard-earned dollars, and harmful lusts that can destroy your life. These all work to drown you in destruction. When you seek to be rich, you're asking for destruction. You become filled with idolatry, which God abhors. You leap right into dangerous and turbulent waters in which many have drowned, pursuing your own destruction by seeking to be rich rather than seeking to build God's kingdom.

"Now wait a moment," you say to yourself. "Certainly the desire for wealth isn't all that bad, is it?"

Well, that all depends on who you listen to, and there are only two voices: the truth of God or the stronghold of the lie. You can choose to accept the testimony of Jesus, John, and Paul, or you can reject it to embrace your own ideas. Jesus said if you seek money you are not seeking His Kingdom nor His righteousness. John said if you love the world or the things of the world, then the love of the Father is not in you. Some may call it "seeking the better life" or "pursuing the American dream," but the Apostle Paul just calls it the love of money.

If you ask people why they try to make a lot of money, they usually say one of two things: either they want to buy something or they want to store more money away. If you can get to the root of it, though, there is one underlying reason for both of them. The person always believes that by doing so he will be filled with more happiness and contentment. The underlying belief? More is better. More is happier. More is greater contentment.

Paul could not disagree more. He said that people who seek money rather than the Kingdom of the Lord and His Righteousness will simply hurt themselves. Rather than happiness, they'll find sorrow. People who believe otherwise are embracing a lie. If they want to get to the truth, they'll need to face this fact: *You cannot fill the void inside of you by stuffing in something from outside.* Money is outside of you while love is an inside thing. Only the Holy Spirit can dwell inside. You can only find peace and fulfillment when your love is directed toward God. A Second Chair individual thinks that enough money will eventually make him happy. He's wrong and he is believing a lie. Paul spoke of Christians who had "strayed from the faith in their greediness...," believers who had wandered from the Lord to seek something else. They forgot that they were called to live for eternity and they began to live for the moment. Their short-sighted focus caused them to stray from the faith. They took their eyes off the Lord to seek something far less valuable.

The love of money is the largest single hindrance to becoming a person in the First Chair. The vast majority of believers in the world today seek just as the Gentiles in Jesus' day did. Their loyalties and their love are not for the Lord, regardless of the seeming intensity of their worship on Sunday morning or Sunday night. Our loyalties and loves are demonstrated more by what happens *between* Sundays than *on* Sundays, and the values and habits of the average church-attending Christian are not statistically very different from the "Gentile" who lives next door. "Gentiles" neither know God nor seek Him, and Christians who live exactly the same way, except for some additional activities on Sunday, are not truly seeking the Lord's Kingdom either.

But, my friend, there is a growing minority who march to a different drummer. They run from those things the Gentiles seek and run toward exactly the opposite goals and objectives. As men of God, First Chair Christians pursue righteousness, godliness, love, patience, and gentleness. Our God is a jealous God. He will have no other gods before Him. The number one god in our culture is money, but the First Chair believer rejects the lie and pursues the true God.

There is a lie that became popular in the early church that still pops up today. It sounds like this: "If you are committed to the Lord, then you will be rich." Many believe that godliness is the pathway to riches, and they hope to attain riches by seeking godliness. That teaching is entirely unbiblical. Paul dismissed this thinking immediately as "useless wranglings of men of corrupt minds and destitute of the truth, *who suppose that godliness is a means of gain*" (1 Timothy 6:5). The Bible teaches that those people who teach that "godliness is a means to financial gain" are themselves destitute of the truth and have a corrupt mind. So what must be the truth? The exact opposite. People who teach that godliness is *not* a means to financial gain are rich with the truth.

I can remember the day as if it were yesterday, though it was more than ten years ago. I was in a hotel room, preparing to speak at a pastors' conference. I traced through the entire Bible what the Lord said to pastors and leaders about money. As I went from one book to the next, something suddenly became incredibly clear: the love of money in the Christian community has been rampant all through history, and it is recorded in the Bible. The Pharisees', "who were lovers of money, also heard all these things" that Jesus said about serving two masters, "and they derided Him" (Luke 16:13-14). That means that they sneered at Him, because they thought they could be spiritual and still love money. Samuel's two sons were judges over Israel after he died, "but his sons did not walk in his ways; *they turned aside after dishonest gain, took bribes*, and perverted justice" (1 Samuel 8:3). The Prophet Micah quotes the Lord as criticizing the leaders of Israel because "*her heads judge for a bribe, her priests teach for pay, and her prophets divine for money*" (Micah 3:9-11). Isaiah quotes the Lord as saying, "Your princes are rebellious, and companions of thieves; *everyone loves bribes*, and follows after rewards. They do not defend the fatherless, nor does the cause of the widow come before them" (Isaiah 1:23).

See it? The love of money has always been there. So when

Jethro gave his son-in-law advice about what kind of leaders he should appoint over Israel, he said, "you shall select from all the people able men, such as fear God, men of truth, *hating covetousness*, and place such over them to be rulers of thousands..." (Exodus 18:21). In Jethro's mind, hating covetousness was an absolute requirement to being a ruler.

Paul continued the same thought in the New Testament: "Do you not know that the unrighteous will not inherit the kingdom of God? Do not be deceived. Neither fornicators, nor idolaters, nor adulterers, nor homosexuals, nor sodomites, nor thieves, nor *covetous*, nor drunkards, nor revilers, nor extortioners will inherit the kingdom of God" (1 Corinthians 6:9-10). Paul even noted that in the end times men will become "lovers of money" (2 Timothy 3:2), and he made sure that elders and deacons in the church were "not covetous" (1 Timothy 3:3).

The lives of Second Chair believers are marked by possessions. First Chair people have moved the focus of their love from possessions to people. They trust in God's provision, invest in God's church, and give to those in need. They make sure their time, talents, and treasures reflect the fact that God is supreme Lord of their lives. They do that by loving people.

STUDY QUESTIONS

1. Why is it important to keep a healthy perspective about these few short years setting the pace for eternity?

2. How is money in competition with God?

3. How can money be someone's master?

4. In what way is seeking money a form of idol worship?

5. How can a Christian move from possessions to people?

Leaving a Legacy

CHAPTER TEN

Raising Godly Children

If I were to ask your children what chair you sit in, what would they say? Have you experienced the power of God in your life, or have you simply heard about it from others? Is God the number one priority in your life, or does He fluctuate somewhere between two and ten? When you are trying to raise kids and you're half-hearted about God, you'll find that your children pick up on the weaker half.

The trouble is, a person may play the part of one who sits in the First Chair—singing in the choir, serving on the church board, or carrying the biggest King James Bible you've ever seen. But they might really be stuck in the Second Chair. A person's attitude about possessions is the best indicator of which Chair they are in. A gal in the First Chair doesn't really care about the car she drives, as long as it gets her where she wants to go. But one in the Second Chair wants to arrive in style: "We've got to get a new car," she'll say, "because this one looks pretty tired." She and her husband might discuss that all the way to church, while the kids sit in the back seat taking it all in. Once the family arrives in the church parking lot, everything changes completely. He suddenly becomes a junior Billy Graham, gently shaking hands with everyone and offering "God bless yous" all around. He might even get up in the service to offer a testimony. His children learn early on that a relationship with God extends only to the edge of the church parking lot.

Imagine a dad who offers a long, flowing prayer when company comes over, but who most of the time simply says, "Dear God, thanks for the food. Amen and pass the meat." Imagine a mom who talks in church about the Bible being the most important book in her life, but whose children never see her read it. It doesn't take long for a child to grasp that the church is filled with hypocrites, that everybody is playing games.

Of course, not everyone in the church *is* playing games. Some people have a dynamic relationship with God, but kids don't know that. The only lives they are really exposed to are the lives of their parents. The only testimonies they hear come from those Second Chair people who talk only about their conversion because they don't have any other first-hand experiences with God. They have beliefs, but not convictions. You can hold a belief, but a conviction holds you, it dominates you. Beliefs are like opinions, and you can share them with your children, though they may reject them. However, you cannot pass on conviction. Conviction is given by the Holy Spirit to the inner man. Each person must establish a personal relationship with God to really have conviction about Him and His priorities.

COMMANDS AND CONSENSUS

My father is a man of convictions. He sat in the First Chair, and saw God work dramatically to change his life. When my dad spoke to me about his Christianity, I knew he had lived his faith. I was one of six kids, and though my dad worked hard to take care of all of us, he took the time regularly to talk with us. Many nights, as I was sitting at our little kitchen table doing my homework, my dad would come in late from work and plop down in the chair across from me so that we could talk. One night I said to him, "Dad, I'm the only guy on the football team who doesn't drink. I want to drink."

He looked at me and smiled. "I can understand that," he said.

"No, you can't," I replied. "You never drink. You and Mom have never taken a drink."

"Well, son, that's not really true. Your Mom and I used to drink all the time."

"What?" I was stunned. "You never told me that!"

"Well, you never asked." So he proceeded to tell me some of the details of his earlier life. "If you'd have known us back then, Son, you would have seen a big cabinet against the wall, filled with liquor bottles. We drank socially. You know Johnny, who lives up the street? When I first became a Christian, I decided to invite Johnny and his wife over for dinner, so I could share the gospel with them. Mom made a big roast, I poured some good red wine, and we told them we'd just become Christians. The next thing I knew, Johnny was standing in the middle of the room, his hat and coat in hand. 'You call yourselves Christians and you're serving liquor?' he bellowed. Then he grabbed his wife's hand and left the house. Your mother and I looked at each other and decided that if liquor was going to put a barrier between us and non-Christians, we'd get rid of the liquor. That night we poured it all down the drain. I've never had a drink since."

"Wow," I said to him, "but...can I drink sometime? Just to see what it's like?"

"Well, Son, that's got to be your choice. You're old enough. But let me ask you a question: Is there a Johnny on your team, watching you?"

As a young man, I got a glimpse into the convictions of a mature Christian. Think about how my father handled that conversation. Had he been sitting in the Second Chair, our discussion would have been remarkably different.

"Dad, I'm thinking of drinking."

"What?!" he would have replied. "You'd better not ever let me catch you drinking!"

"Why not?"

"Because I said so, that's why not."

"Well, I'm going to do it anyway."

"What will the people at church think if you get caught drinking?"

Of course, this issue has nothing to do with the people at church, but a Second Chair person is more interested in what the church will think than in what God will think. A First Chair father has convictions based on the Bible. If the Scripture says to do something, he does it. If it says to refrain from it, he refrains. He is most concerned with the *commands of Scripture*. A Second Chair father doesn't think that way. His major concern is with the *consensus of Christians*. The man concerned with the commands of Scripture sets an example of holiness in all areas of his life; the one concerned with the consensus of Christians sets an example of hypocrisy.

The First Chair mother has a *relationship* with God, and it impacts every part of her life. When she sees a need, her first thought is to take it to the Lord in prayer. The Second Chair mother has a *responsibility* to God, and that's how she approaches her faith in Christ. She knows she should go to church, and she knows she should donate some time to a ministry, so she fulfills her obligation. But if you follow her around, you'll find out that the only time she talks to God is to say, "Thanks for the food," and that will be only if somebody is watching. If you have a relationship with God, your children will become Christians; if you have a responsibility to God, your kids will get turned off by the demands of "religion." It seems funny, but it has been my experience that Second Chair parents are the ones who are always spouting off Proverbs 22:6: "Train up a child in the way he should go, and when he is old he will not turn from it." Unfortunately, you can't train a child in the way he should go unless you are sitting in the First Chair.

CHRIST'S CALL TO CHRISTIANS

Paul warned a group of people in one church that there were some who were spiritual, some who were carnal, and some who were natural or unsaved. That is, in every church there are some people who really know God, some who know about Him, and some who don't know Him at all.

In Revelation 3:15 Christ gives a clarion call to Christians. This is a passage that most people have only a surface understanding of. Christ is speaking to Christians when He says, "I know your deeds, that you are neither cold nor hot. I wish you were one or the other!"

Did you ever stop to ask yourself, "Why?" Why does Jesus want us to be cold or hot? The person sitting in the Second Chair stands between the First Chair and the Third, keeping them apart. The guy in the First Chair has a message to share with that lost soul in the Third Chair, but the person in the middle often gets in the way! His weak faith hinders the process of evangelism and it keeps people out of the kingdom. So Jesus says, "Because you are luke-warm—neither hot nor cold—I am about to spit you out of my mouth. You say, 'I am rich; I have acquired wealth and do not need a thing.' But you do not realize that you are wretched, pitiful, poor, blind, and naked. I counsel you to buy from me gold refined in the fire, so you can become rich" (Revelation 3:16-18).

Jesus is speaking to Christians in this passage. This doesn't mean that He will kick people out of His family; what it means is that their behavior is repugnant to Him. The people in the First Chair are sold out to God. The next group starts sold out to God but becomes more concerned with possessions, position, prestige, and power. Something else takes the priority rather than God. Jesus warns us, "Those whom I love I rebuke and discipline" (v. 19a). He loves us, but He will not stand for our being lukewarm. Christ's call is clear: "Be earnest and repent. Here I am! I stand at the door and knock. If anyone hears my voice and opens the door, I will go in and eat with him, and he with me" (vv. 19b-20).

Repentance is getting up off that Second Chair, confessing your spiritual lukewarmness, and moving over to the First Chair. We need to repent of taking God for granted. We often use this passage as an evangelistic message, but the primary message is that Christ is knocking on the hearts of *believers*. *He wants you to know that it is possible to have a dynamic walk with God. You can move to the First Chair!*

In your mind's eye, picture yourself standing up from that Second Chair and moving with courage and boldness to the First Chair. Now visualize yourself sitting down and enjoying the comfort of that chair. You know why it's comfortable? Because it's the Lord's chair, and it's where you belong. It was meant to be yours. You must ask forgiveness and start fresh in your walk with the Lord.

HOW FAMILY LEGACIES ARE CREATED

The principle of the Three Chairs isn't limited to just families. Nations go through that same process, as do churches, denominations, Bible colleges, and ministries. They start out in the First Chair, totally committed to Christ, full of the work of the Holy Spirit. They give way to a "generation" that is sitting in the Second Chair, that knows Christ and has heard what the Lord has done in the past, but has no personal experience with the works of God. They aren't able to tell what powerful thing God has done in their own lives, so they have little to pass on to the third generation. That generation, the "grandchildren," sit in the Third Chair, not knowing Christ as Savior. They don't know about the mighty work God has done in the past. They were never told, for fear they would ask the questions, "Why isn't God at work now? What about us? How come the Lord doesn't work like that for you?"

The challenge for the church is to get people who are sitting in the Second Chair to move to the First Chair. You see, people who are the sons and daughters of First Chair Christians learn all the truths about God. They generally believe what their parents believe, until they make a break in high school or college and try to determine which part of their faith is their own. As a child you don't know how to think different from what you have been told. But as you get older you begin to test the beliefs of your parents. Your folks can tell you what they believe, but you want your own experience with God. If you never have an experience with Him, you'll have nothing to pass on to your children. You can teach them the Scriptures, and you can tell them the lessons, but wisdom comes from experience.

For example, many of us grew up in homes where the family had devotions together every day. But once we left home, we never practiced daily devotions. Do you know why that is? Because *you weren't having devotions; your parents were having them for you.* Your parents had a conviction about the importance of daily time in the Word, but you never developed that conviction for yourself.

That's why the second generation is where the cause of Christ is either won or lost. They will either decide to move to the First Chair and experience total commitment to Christ, or they will remain in the Second Chair and allow their faith to wither away.

THE CHAIR OF BONDAGE

Nobody sits in the First Chair all the time. Most of us would say that it's our desire to be there most of the time, but the fact is that we have a tendency to slide over into the Second Chair. Ambition, possessions, and power creep into our lives, and pretty soon we're thinking more about ourselves than about God, and we've plopped down into the Second Chair without realizing it. John tells us that those worldly things get in the way—the lust of the flesh, the lust of the eyes, and the pride of life. But he also warns us that these things "come not from the Father but from the world" (1 John 2:16). When you turn your attention to those worldly things, you compromise your convictions as a First Chair person.

Too many people have bought into the world's concept of "success." I often talk with working mothers who claim they "have to work" if they are going to pay their bills. But when you look at the bills, you often see that they represent the values of this materialistic culture. They want to have a nice home, so they spend their time at work rather than with their children. They want nice cars, nice furniture, and nice clothes for everyone, so they "have to work to meet the needs." But that's an argument based on materialism, not Scripture. It's an argument based on a lie. In actuality, truth is that unless both parents work they cannot live according to their *wants*. Though God has promised to provide for our needs, they choose not to be content with that.

The Second Chair is a chair of bondage. It binds people into a selfish lifestyle. It keeps them bound up through debt, mortgages, and a constant desire for *more*. We all know what that feels like. Let's say your station wagon is getting a little tired. It uses a bit of oil, there are stains on the seat, and the style is a bit outdated. What you really want is a mini-van, with a bit more room and a more modern appearance. You dream about it, plan for it, and finally the day comes when you actually take possession of a new mini-van. It can carry the kids and all their junk, it drives like a dream, and it looks great in your driveway. You're perfectly satisfied with that mini-van, and you feel fulfilled...for a while. Then one day somebody at the mall opens his door into it and leaves a dent. The kids spill grape soda on the carpet. The water pump breaks and it has to go in for repairs. It isn't very long and your mini-van isn't making you feel fulfilled any more. So you have to go get something else to return that feeling of satisfaction to your life. And the cycle starts all over again.

Our culture is based on consumption. We are deluged with advertising that tells you that you aren't complete in some way, and that the product being offered is the one that will complete you. Your teeth aren't white enough, your hair isn't bouncy enough, and your automobile isn't classy enough, so you need to buy a new product to will fill that "need." Our society is based on this kind of thinking, and people in the Second Chair have become part of its system. It's a chair of bondage.

THE CHAIR OF SUBMISSION

God's Word warns us that "the world and its desires pass away, but the man who does the will of God lives forever" (1 John 2:17). Too many Christians spend all their time dreaming, scheming, and steaming over temporal things, things that won't last. John reminds us that it is eternal things that are to be on the hearts and minds of God's people. Rather than worrying about what the *world* wants, we ought to be concerned with what *God* wants. That's why James reminds us that "friendship with the world is hatred toward God" (James 4:4), and Paul exhorts us to "be not conformed to the pattern of this world, but be transformed by the renewing of your mind" (Romans 12:2).

Though we live in it, Christians are not part of this world or its system. If Satan is the "god of this world" (2 Corinthians 4:4), we ought to reject the system and turn to the One True God. Jesus, in the Sermon on the Mount, encourages people to not focus on the riches of this world: "Do not store up for yourselves treasures on earth where moth and rust destroy, and where thieves break in and steal. But store up for yourselves treasures in heaven, where moth and rust do not destroy, and where thieves do not break in. For where your treasure is, there your heart will be also" (Matthew 6:19-21). Christ knew that your earthly investments reveal your heavenly commitments. Those who sit in the Second Chair have hearts that are concerned with this world, but those in the First Chair have hearts that are concerned with the people of this world and with the will of God.

The First Chair is a chair of submission. The people who sit in it submit to the will of God, *even though they know it will ostracize them from the world* because the world doesn't understand God or His ways. In fact, it hates God, which is why they killed His Son. And "if the world hates you, keep in mind it hated me first," the Lord said to His disciples in the upper room on the day He was crucified. "If you belonged to the world, it would love you as its own.

As it is, you do not belong to the world, but I have chosen you out of the world. That is why the world hates you" (John 15:18-19).

Have you ever considered yourself hated by this world? Christ himself said that when you represent Him, that's what happens. Christians in the First Chair submit themselves to God, regardless of the outcome in this world.

Those who sit in the Second Chair don't want to be hated by the world. They want to be loved by the world, and they do all sorts of things to compromise so that they'll be accepted. God's priorities are not their priorities, and when their children see them talking about the right things but living the wrong values, those children live in conflict.

If you sit in the First Chair, you see Scripture as the only truth. The Bible guides your life and your actions. But if you spend much of your life in the Second Chair, you begin to see the Bible as being quaint, or dated. You ignore passages that are inconvenient to your lifestyle. For example, much of the Christian community in our culture is being subverted by television. On TV, everything having to do with God is mocked and criticized. Immorality and sexual innuendo is everywhere. Yet the average Christian adult in this country watches thirty-two hours of television per week (and claims to be too busy to take a position of service in the church). You see, the Second Chair is full of compromise, but the First Chair is full of obedience to God.

THE REBUKE OF GOD

It's time for Christians in our culture to wake up to the fact that we are sliding down a long, slippery slope of compromise. We live in a culture with an embarrassment of riches, and we think that we are pretty well off. We think we are rich because we have acquired so many possessions, but Jesus says to us, "You say, 'I am rich; I have acquired wealth and do not need a thing.' But you do no realize that you are wretched, pitiful, poor, blind, and naked" (Revelation 3:17).

Some people have mistaken material wealth for the blessing of God. They think that earthly riches is a sign of God's pleasure with us. What nonsense! Didn't Jesus say, after meeting the rich young ruler, that it is easier for a camel to go through the eye of a needle than for a rich man to enter the kingdom of God? The rich reject God because they don't feel their need for Him, or because they aren't willing to surrender all to the Almighty. Now, if it is difficult for a rich man to get into heaven, then most of us in modern day America are going to have a really tough time. We live in one of the wealthiest times ever. The average American's income ranks in the top five percent of the world's economy. We have so many possessions that we have had to start an entirely new industry, the self-storage structure, simply to contain all our extra stuff. The *average* American homeowner can't fit his belongings into his personal dwelling—and that's probably unprecedented in world history.

So when Jesus warns of the difficulties for the rich to get into heaven, He's talking about us. He is rebuking us, and warning us of our lifestyle. "No one can serve two masters. Either he will hate the one and love the other, or he will be devoted to the one and despise the other. You cannot serve both God and money" (Matthew 6:24). The love for money and the desire for popularity with the world are the two great motivators for people in the Second Chair. But the choices we make on this earth have eternal consequences.

Jesus Christ demands action. If you are going to choose to leave a godly legacy, your values will have to be revealed in your actions so that your children can *see* your commitment to Christ, not just hear about it. Your life's influence on your kids will imprint them forever. What heritage do you want to pass on?

CREATING A GODLY LEGACY

We are called as Christian parents to leave a godly legacy. Moses emphasized how important it is to the family that the parents have a love for God:

"Hear, O Israel: The Lord our God, the Lord is one. Love the Lord your God with all your heart and with all your soul and with all your strength. These commandments that I give you today are to be upon your hearts. *Impress them on your children.* Talk about them when you sit at home and when you walk along the road, when you lie down and when you get up. Tie them as symbols on your hands and bind them on your foreheads. Write them on the door frames of your houses and on your gates" (Deuteronomy 6:4-9).

If you want to leave a legacy, *love God.* Make your love for Him visible. Talk about the Lord with your kids. Take a stand for God in a culture that hates holiness. Sit in the First Chair and experience the life-changing power of the Lord in your life, and you will set an example for them to follow. If you stay in the Second Chair and merely tell your kids about what God *could* do, you don't give them a chance to actually see God at work.

I have had parents tell me, "I trained up my child in the way he should go, and God isn't keeping His promise!" I often wonder if those parents have a vital *relationship* with God, or if they simply have accepted the *religion* surrounding Him. You see, when you sit in the First Chair, you become emotionally passionate about God.

Half of all Christian marriages are in serious trouble these days. Those difficulties impact the children, and cast a shadow over their legacy. Most of those troubled marriages will eventually produce troubled children. The reason behind the trouble, I think, is that the parents are sitting in the wrong Chairs. If you take a seat in the Second Chair, you'll develop problems because you are not living a life of integrity. Your marriage will develop problems. Eventually, your family will, too.

If you really want to overcome those troubles, you need to become a First Chair believer, putting Jesus first. Let Him unleash His power and change your life. Your spouse will see it, and your relationship will change. Your children will see it, and they'll be changed. You *can* leave a godly legacy. One is created by establishing Jesus Christ as the center of your life, and letting Him change the way you live.

But be warned: it won't always be easy. He calls you to service. He calls you to commitment. He might call you to significantly change your lifestyle. But as your children see you change, as they see something significant and eternal take hold of your life, they will begin to understand the reality of God, and want Him in their own lives. When they do, your godly legacy will be established.

As we have already seen, Moses sat in the First Chair, loving and serving God as he led the nation of Israel. When Moses grew old, he left his country in the hands of Joshua, who also had a vibrant relationship with God. Joshua experienced the power of the Lord throughout his life, and credited his many victories to God's intervention. When Joshua's life drew to a close, he too wanted to ensure that his country would always remember and revere the Lord. He gathered all the people together, and he reminded them that, though their ancestors had been pagans, God had chosen the Jews to bless all nations and had accomplished great things on their behalf. Joshua exhorted everyone to remain true to the Lord. "But if serving the Lord seems undesirable to you, then choose for yourselves this day whom you will serve, whether the gods your forefathers served beyond the River, or the gods of the Amorites, in whose land you are living. But as for me and my household, we will serve the Lord" (Joshua 24:15). Joshua knew who the King is. He knew the importance of remaining faithful to God, and of sitting in the First Chair with the heavenly Father.

There is no passage in Scripture where God says, "Try to obey me." God is interested in results, not just intentions. He instructs us to reach all nations, and He expects us to do just that. He instructs us to raise godly kids, and He won't be satisfied with having us respond, "Well, Lord, we gave it a try." You can't be a First Chair person unless you commit to developing First Chair children. If you don't disciple your children toward godliness, you will "inoculate" them against the things of the Spirit.

In the medical field, inoculation is when the doctor gives you enough of the germs, usually the flu, to help your body build up a resistance to the disease. That keeps you from getting sick when the flu season hits. Christian parents can spiritually inoculate their children against the things of God by giving them just enough of the rules and regulations without sharing the joy and vibrancy of the Holy Spirit. The children learn that God is real but church is boring and Christianity is a series of rules to follow. They become resistant to the things of God, and they wind up spending their lives in the Second or Third Chair.

Raising godly children is your responsibility, Christian parent. You cannot delegate it to the youth pastor, to the Sunday School teacher, or even to God Himself. He gave them to *you*, and He's going to hold you responsible. There is no blaming the world, the television, the school, or the peer group for failures. Those are all significant circumstances, but they don't change the command of God to parents.

Many people seem to think it's impossible to raise godly kids in this age, but I don't buy that. Our society isn't the most godless the world has ever seen, and there are plenty of parents successfully raising godly children in spite of the culture. It's their responsibility. Granted, it's a tough job. I think it's the toughest task anyone can take on, and it seems to foster a feeling of failure in many. I don't feel competent to do it all of the time, but the Lord hasn't instructed me to feel competent. He's just ordered me to do it. I make mistakes, but the fact remains that the one thing I want to accomplish in my family is leaving a godly legacy.

Now, what are some of the ways we can do that?

PRAY WITH YOUR CHILDREN.

Late one night, my son and I took a walk together. We were talking about things that were important to us, and praying as we walked. At that time we had a pregnant gal living with us, whom we were trying to help. As our prayers turned toward that young lady's troubles, my son suddenly said, "You know, Dad, she's not saved."

"I know," I replied, looking at my watch. It was getting late, almost 11 p.m.

"What if we were to pray that she trusts Christ tonight?" he asked me.

"I think that's a good idea, Son."

"Do you think she'll still be up?"

"Well," I replied, "She's pretty tired. I doubt it." Then I looked at my boy and asked, "What do you want to do?"

"I think we should pray and ask God to keep her up, so that we can talk to her."

So we prayed for that very thing as we walked the rest of the way home. I made sure he was the one to ask, because I wanted him to know what it's like to sit in the First Chair. He said something like, "Lord, keep her up. Help her to trust Christ when we get home tonight." Meanwhile, I was praying silently, asking the Lord to use this opportunity to build the faith of my boy. As we walked through the door of our home, the young lady was standing in the living room. "I don't know what's wrong," she said to us. "I just can't get to sleep."

My son looked at me and smiled. And she gave her heart to Jesus that very night.

Have you ever noticed how Christian parents are sometimes afraid to pray for big things with their children? They'll pray for "safe" things, things they know will probably happen whether they pray or not.

"Give Grandpa a safe trip."

"Help Suzy get over her cold."

"Take care of all of us."

And of course there's nothing *wrong* with praying for those things. We are encouraged in Scripture to pray at all times, on all occasions, with all kinds of requests. But it doesn't take much faith to pray for things that we know will probably turn out all right, and it does little for building the faith of our children. I think the reason behind this sort of praying is that parents are worried that the faith of their kids will be shattered if they pray for something great and it doesn't come to pass. But if we don't believe in a God who has the power to do great things, why bother praying at all? If God can't supernaturally work in a situation, what are we doing wasting our time in church on Sundays? We could be home catching all the games on television!

But we *do* have a supernatural, prayer-answering God. He knows what we need, and He is waiting for us to ask Him to work in our lives. My editor, Dr. Chip MacGregor, told me a story about praying with his three-year-old son when they went to pick up Mrs. MacGregor at a big conference center. Pulling into a taxi zone, Chip realized he only had a few minutes to find his wife in vast crowd.

His young son, recognizing the problem, said, "Well, why don't we pray?" Then he folded his little hands and say, "Dear Jesus, help us find Mommy right away!" As he looked up, the crowd seemed to part and his mother came walking straight toward them.

"It worked!" the boy cried. "God answered my prayer!"

Faith is built from those kinds of situations. It wasn't the father who received the answer to prayer, but the son. Prayer will help your children experience First Chair things.

Asaph, the psalmist, said to his people:

"O my people, hear my teaching; listen to the words of my mouth. I will open my mouth in parables, I will utter things hidden from of old—things we have heard and known, things our fathers told us. *We will not hide them from their children; we will tell the next generation the praiseworthy deeds of the Lord, His power, and the wonders He has done*" (Psalm 78:1-4).

Remember, the people in the First Chair experience the works of God for themselves. The people in the Second Chair don't, but they know about the works. The people in the Third Chair don't even know about the works of the Lord. It is your responsibility to share His works with your children in such a way that they have their own experiences. Pray with them for God to do great things. Tell them about the answers to prayer you have seen recently. Your example will lead them to a First Chair experience of their own.

TELL YOUR CHILDREN THE STORIES OF GOD.

It is God's will that you teach the Bible to your kids. To fail to do so is disobedience. You've got to get into the habit of storytelling with your children, so that they know what God has done in the past.

Children love stories. Stories take a complex world and turn it into bite-sized chunks. Kids come to understand the world through stories. That's why little ones will want to hear the same story time after time. When my children were little, I'd read a favorite book to them. As soon as I got to the end and closed the book, they'd reach over and open it to the beginning again, expecting me to repeat the story immediately. Parents might get sick of hearing the same old story again and again, but that's how children learn.

If you want your children to learn about God, *tell them the stories of God.* Do you remember all those great Old Testament stories you learned in Sunday School? Teach them to your children, over and over. The parables of Jesus? Let your kids hear them. The stories about Jesus' life? Repeat them again and again so that your kids understand the uniqueness of Christ.

Asaph had more to say in Psalm 78:

"He decreed statutes for Jacob and established the law in Israel,

Which *He commanded our forefathers to teach their children,*

So the next generation would know them, even the children yet to be born.

And they in turn would tell their children.

Then they would put their trust in God

And would not forget His deeds

But would keep His commands" (vs.5-7).

Too many Americans have stopped the ritual of story-telling. Families used to keep their stories alive so that the younger generations knew what it was like for the ancestors "back in old country." Many families told of being related to famous Americans, fighting in the Civil War, or going through Ellis Island when they immigrated. We've stopped doing that, maybe because we have no regard for the past or maybe just because we take it all for granted. But we ought to be telling the stories, especially the stories of God, until the kids cry out, "Wait! Let *me* tell it this time!" When they hear it enough times, they'll be able to relate it to their own kids, and the legacy can be passed on to another generation.

Asaph's point was that if you tell your children the stories of God they will put their trust in God. According to John, God's words were written specifically so that we would believe that Jesus is the Christ, the Son of God. Tell your children the stories of God's Word, and trust that it will have that effect on them.

People who sit in the First Chair are familiar with God's Word. Let your kids see you reading it. Make sure they hear you and your spouse talking about it, so that they know you use Scripture as part of your regular interaction with others. Let them know you're thinking about the things of God. When they see how highly you value God's perspectives on life as expressed in the Bible, they will value its wisdom too. But they must *see* you interacting with Scripture. If they hear you *talk about* reading the Bible, but never see you *do* it, they'll figure it's just another good intention, like not watching too much television or limiting yourself to one piece of pie. There's a big difference between a good intention and actual obedience. If you want to raise godly children, read your Bible. It's like putting them in your lap as you sit in the First Chair. They can see how important and powerful God's Word is to you, and they'll want that for themselves.

SET A GODLY EXAMPLE FOR YOUR CHILDREN.

Let's face it: if you really want to raise godly kids, you're going to have to lead a godly life. You can't fake a spiritual life and have that example somehow blossom into real holiness in the lives of your children. Parenting is hard work, so you might as well decide now whether or not you're serious about your walk with Christ. Moses tells us in Deuteronomy 4:9 to "be careful and watch yourselves closely so that you do not forget the things your eyes have seen or let them slip from your heart as long as you live."

That's the core issue of being a First Chair parent: if you keep yourself close to God, you'll try to nurture your children's relationship to Him. If you're in the Second Chair, you don't have much to say to your kids about God. You don't really know the thoughts of God, since you only read the Bible when you have to. You have nothing to pass on as your legacy.

Moses goes on to say, "Teach them to your children and to their children after them" (Deuteronomy 4:9b). It's your job to help your children understand God, and you can't teach what you don't know. Moreover, it's your job to help your *grandchildren* know God.

My kids have terrific grandparents. My folks take our kids away for a long weekend once a year. We call it "grandparent's weekend," and we've been doing it for years. Everyone who attends has to lead a devotional. They spend their time talking about the faith. They discuss what it means to be a Wilkinson. What do we believe? What do we stand for? They tell family stories, so the kids get a sense of history. I think it's one of the most important things that happens each year.

Moses reminds the people of Israel, "Remember the day you stood before the Lord your God at Horeb, when He said to me, 'Assemble the people before me to hear my words so that they may learn to revere me as long as they live in the land and may teach them to their children'" (Deuteronomy 4:10). In other words, *keep those important stories in your mind.* Tell your children how you became a Christian. Tell them of your significant spiritual experiences. Keep track of answered prayers, and rejoice over them as a family. As they get older, show them how you read Scripture, and what you do in your prayer closet. Talk about the things you are learning from the Bible. Let them see that Christianity isn't just what happens on Sunday mornings, but it is a constant relationship between you and the Lord Jesus Christ. Then they'll know what it's like to sit in the First Chair and they won't be satisfied with a Second Chair existence.

TALK TO YOUR CHILDREN ABOUT SPIRITUAL THINGS.

I love the Lord Jesus Christ. He is present with me at all times, and I want my life to reflect Him. Jesus is part of my conversation with others. His name often comes up. Jesus is also part of my thought process, and before making decisions I spend time with Him. A First Chair person tries to be in constant communication with the Savior.

As a parent, my goal is to reveal my relationship with Christ to my children so that they can establish a similar relationship. Deuteronomy Chapter 6, a passage we have already looked at, offers four principles on how to do that:

> "Love the Lord your God with all your heart and with all your soul and with all your strength. These commandments that I give you today are to be upon your hearts. Impress them on your children. Talk about them when you sit at home and when you walk along the road, when you lie down, and when you get up. Tie them as symbols on your foreheads. Write them on the door frames of your houses and on your gates" (Deuteronomy 6:5-9).

The first principle is that *I need to impress the truth of God on my kids.* That is, I need to teach them about God from the Bible and my own experience. The word translated "impress" was often used in making pottery. When the clay was still soft, the potter could use a sharp tool to make impressions on his work of art. He might carve a fancy design, or press pieces of colorful stone into the clay. Then, as the clay aged, it became hard and permanently took on the impressions the potter had made. Our children are like clay. We are to impress upon them the truth of God while they are still young. Then as they grow up, those impressions will remain a part of their lives. As you talk to your children, impress them with the truth of God.

The second thing that passage suggests is that *I need to talk with them at various times about God*. Find various times in the day to work your love of God into the conversation. Talk about Him when you get up in the morning, and when you go to bed. Let God be part of your conversation when you share a meal, when you're traveling in the car, and when you're just sitting around the house. This doesn't mean that you need to turn every event of your life into an object lesson. Moses isn't suggesting that you ladle on the spiritual truth in some sort of artificial manner. He is saying that those who sit in the First Chair make God part of their normal conversation, and we are to include our kids in it. If He has blessed you, tell your family. If He has revealed something to you during your quiet time, talk to your kids about it. If there is a godly principle that speaks to the moment at hand, use it as you discuss the situation. Make God part of your discussions about what videos to watch and which books to read. If God is Lord of all your life, there is no limit to the way you can talk about Him.

Moses points out that we should be talking and teaching our kids all the time, and that requires a bit of planning. I encourage parents to figure out what they need to be working on with their kids. What are the areas in which your children need to grow? Plan to talk about those things in the normal course of conversation.

Remember, you are parenting all the time. When I was a young man I didn't understand that. I figured my time at home was *my* time. But I matured and realized that I was being selfish and neglecting my responsibility. When I leave the office I am no longer CEO of an organization, but I do take on the role of father when I step in the door of my home. I spend my time at home raising godly kids. It's funny, but between work, parenting, fostering my relationship to my wife, and my own spiritual growth, there isn't much time left for anything else! But that's how it's going to be if you want to fulfill the biblical responsibility of being a parent. You have to die to self. Your flesh is tired and wants to just relax, and you feel that you deserve it. But if you get into the habit of "zoning out," you'll find you aren't doing your job as a parent. Sure, everybody needs a little time away, and I encourage you to plan some into your schedule so that you can get your batteries recharged every now and again. But *your* needs will take second place to the needs of your kids.

Talk to your children. Many parents never do really communicate with their kids, and it causes all kinds of problems when their little kids become teens. Suddenly there's rebellion and a total lack of communication. So *turn off the television and talk.* Agree to shut it off for a month and see what happens. Or limit TV watching to weekends only, and see if you don't converse more as a family.

Parents usually want to talk at mealtimes, because the entire family is together. But kids are more prone to talk at bedtime when it's just the two of you. So turn off the TV, go sit on their bed, and talk. Show them you're committed to communicating with them. You don't have to say much, just ask them about their day and let them share what's going on in their lives. You'll find out what they need and what struggles they are facing. They are your kids and they need to learn from you.

The third thing Deuteronomy 6 tells us is that *I need to display my faith to my children.* Moses spoke of "binding signs to the forehead," which was an Old Testament method for showing what you believed in. The Jews would actually put Scripture passages in a small box and tie it around their heads so that it rested on the forehead. When you saw them, you knew what they stood for. The idea is to show your children that you aren't afraid to be recognized as a Christian. Maybe there's a bumper sticker on your car, or a pin in your lapel, or a logo on your business card that identifies you as a

Christian. Perhaps you marched in the pro-life rally or wrote a letter to the editor that took a stand for Christian values. Let your children know that you are proud to be identified with Christ.

Once, when my family went a restaurant, my daughter, Jenny, suddenly pointed to another family.

"Dad! Look at those people over there!"

I looked over to see a woman who sat alone with five kids, their heads bowed in prayer. "What about them?"

"I've never seen anybody pray in a restaurant besides us!" she replied.

Sometimes young people can feel out of place, that it's "weird" to be Christians in an un-Christian world. Help them to understand that you're *proud* to be a Christian, and that you *want* to be identified with Christ. Later they'll understand that God's people have always been persecuted, because this world hates God. But that means we're identifying ourselves with Jesus Christ. The world hated Him, too.

What do people see when they watch you? First Chair Christians aren't afraid to be identified with Christ, even though it's out of place with the world.

The fourth principle in that passage from Deuteronomy is that *I am to make my home honoring to God*. Moses talks about writing God's truth on the doors and gates of our homes. Think about it: when people look around your home, what do they see? What books do they see on your shelves? What movies are sitting beside the VCR? What's playing on the radio? Can people who enter there sense they are in a Christian home? Make your house a temple for the Lord. Create an environment that fosters spiritual development. This makes talking about spiritual things easier and more natural in your family. First Chair Christians display their hearts for God by talking to their children.

NEVER GIVE UP ON YOUR CHILDREN.

As a parent, your responsibility doesn't end when your children turn eighteen. They're your kids forever, and God says they remain your legacy. Not long ago I was talking with a man who's daughter had an affair, left her spouse, and filed for divorce. He was just torn up about it, but I'll tell you what that brother did. He went to work. He and his wife flew down to meet with her. They got her involved with other relatives. They counseled her, and eventually they brought about a restoration in the marriage. I have deep respect for that man, because in most cases in our culture, the parents would simply have shaken their heads and sadly watched the events proceed. Your children remain yours forever—don't give up on them. Just because they reach eighteen, or move out of the house, doesn't mean you stop parenting.

I think that's the real message of Deuteronomy Chapter 6. It offers us help with the nitty-gritty of Christian parenting: "These are the commands, decrees and laws the Lord your God directed me to teach you to observe in the land that you are crossing the Jordan to possess, so that you, your children, and their children after them may fear the Lord your God as long as you live by keeping all His decrees and commands that I give you, and so that you may enjoy long life" (Deuteronomy 6:1-2).

All of time is linked together in God's mind; He sees the entire scene from beginning to end and into eternity. The reason He waits to judge mankind is that the impact of our lives does not cease when we die. He waits until the full influence of every person, for good or evil, is complete. Parents will be judged—it's their responsibility to raise godly children. Did we help our children understand the Lord? Did we tell them the stories of God? Did we set a godly example before them, so that they know what a mature Christian is? Godly parents are the key to godly children.

I'm constantly amazed at people who sit in the Second Chair and wonder why their kids don't love God. Some of them have devotions with their kids, some even send them to Christian schools, but they've never figured out that their personal example outweighs any other factor. Do you love the Lord with all your heart, soul, mind, and strength? First Chair people do. And they continue to set that example, no matter how old their children are.

Are you leaving a legacy of godly children? If you want to see your kids choose to sit in the First Chair, help them experience First Chair things. Pray with them. Take them on activities with you so they can see how a mature Christian behaves. Develop a ministry that you and your kids can do together. Ask them to give a testimony. Encourage them by putting them in leadership positions. Have them help you when you're asked to serve. Send them on mission trips, which is perhaps the most significant spiritual tool God uses with young people. All of these things reveal the First Chair life to them. And that will cause them to become a godly legacy, which is the goal of Christian parenting.

STUDY QUESTIONS

1. In your own words, what is the difference between a First Chair parent and a Second Chair parent?

2. How is the Second Chair a chair of bondage for a Christian?

3. Why is it important to pray with our children?

4. How do stories build our children's faith?

5. What three things could you do to set a First Chair example to your children?

CHAPTER ELEVEN

The First-Chair Father

A father who wants to develop children who love the Lord will have to sit in the First Chair. He'll have to love his wife, lead his family, commit to his kids, and genuinely love Jesus and rely on Him.

A few months ago our kids had some college friends over to our house. They spent the evening with us, talking and laughing and playing games with Darlene and myself. Just as they were leaving to head back to campus, one of the young ladies took my wife and me aside and asked, "Can I talk with you for a minute in private?"

To be honest, we didn't know what to expect. I thought perhaps she had a relationship problem that she wanted to discuss, or maybe a question about something to do with our family. Instead she just stood in the kitchen, looking at Darlene and I holding hands, tears welling in her eyes.

"Thank you," she finally choked out.

"You're welcome. You are always welcome to come to our home."

"No," she said, "what I mean to say is, thanks for holding hands."

Darlene and I looked at each other. We weren't sure what the gal was trying to say.

"This is the way a house is supposed to be," she continued. "The way I've always pictured it. There aren't many left anymore."

It was like a whack on the side of my head. Imagine—a young person thanking a middle-aged guy for having a happy marriage! You know, there really aren't that many happy marriages out there. There is a sense of frustration in our society; we wonder if anybody is ever satisfied and fulfilled in marriage. Even in the church, there is a dearth of healthy, vibrant marriages, and I think it's because we've missed God's plan for a happy marriage.

Men, the key to having a happy marriage is *you*. It's really that simple. If the man will do his job the way God intended, he'll find his wife willing to submit and ready to satisfy. But if the husband fails to do what God instructs him to do, the marriage will be tense and unfulfilling. Let's take a look at what the Lord had to say to the first man.

THE PLAN OF GOD

In Genesis 2:15, God puts the man in charge of this world. "Then the Lord God took the man, and put him in the garden of Eden to tend and keep it. And the Lord commanded the man, saying, 'Of every tree of the garden you may freely eat, but of the tree of the knowledge of good and evil you shall not eat. For in the day that you eat, you shall surely die.'" God makes Adam head over everything in the world. Then in the very next verse, the Lord says, "It is not good that man should be alone. I will make him a helper suitable for him." From the very beginning, God set up a system with a *head* and a *helper*.

The Old Testament used the word *head* to define the husband's role on several occasions. The word literally means "the prominent one," and was used to describe the prow on a ship, the highest point on a mountain, and the master who has authority over everyone on a farm. To be the head means you will take charge of your family.

The Apostle Paul put it this way: "Wives, submit to your own husbands as unto the Lord *for the husband is the head of the wife, just as Christ is the head of the church*" (Ephesians 5:22-23).

Jesus, of course, is the ultimate head of the church. He founded it, He is its unchallenged leader, and He goes to great lengths to protect it. In the same way the husband is the head of his family. He is the leader, to be respected by all, and he is to work hard to protect his family from any threats. That doesn't mean he's a despot, sitting in an easy chair and proclaiming his selfish desires· the rule of law. As God's leader, he is active, leading by both example and direction.

The frustration for so many wives is not that their husband isn't the head, it's that *he isn't the leader*. He doesn't rule. He doesn't take charge. He doesn't initiate. A head of household who is passive isn't a leader, and he isn't following God's plan. That has led many women to reject God's plan for families, claiming that it demeans women. The Lord said this would happen at the fall of mankind, when He told Eve, "I will greatly increase your pains in childbearing; with pain you will give birth to children. Your desire will be for your husband, and he will rule over you" (Genesis 3:16). Those words literally mean that the woman will desire her husband's place as head of the household. It's part of the fall of man. Husbands are called to lead, but if they fail to do so, the wife will try to step in. Again, all this happens because we don't fulfill the perfect plan of God.

WHY DON'T HUSBANDS LEAD?

If you talk with a man privately, he'll admit that he wants to be the leader in his home. You don't have to convince a husband to want to lead; in their hearts, all men already want to. Yet it often doesn't happen. I think there are three wrong beliefs in the minds of husbands that keep them from leading.

First, most husbands believe *they don't know enough to lead*. They've never led before. They haven't been down that road, so how on earth are they supposed to know? Many men think to themselves, "I'm not sure what to do," so they do nothing. And wives think, "Well, if he won't, I will!"

The problem is that the husband believes the misconception that a good leader knows everything, all the time. That simply isn't true. All good leaders face situations that are new to them. All good leaders feel stumped sometimes. But it is wrong to believe you shouldn't lead because you don't know how to. God has called you to lead, so lead anyway—even if you don't know it all!

A second wrong belief goes like this: "I can't lead because *I don't feel very confident leading.*" They don't have that sense of assurance, the confidence to be able to say, "Follow me." Insecurity keeps them from obeying God. They don't know where to go, and they don't know if their wives will want to go with them when they do go. And they feel that they'll get blamed if anything goes wrong. They reason that the best way to keep away from all those dangers is simply to not lead.

This belief is based entirely on fear. What the husband is really saying is, "I'm afraid of leading." But the Bible tells us to fear not, for God is with us, no matter what the fear is. Take courage, men, the Lord is on your side. New circumstances will always be fearful for a leader, but we are called to have faith in God and lead anyway. In a marriage, there is going to be insecurity and unknown problems—you can count on it. You'll feel fear. But courage means to do it in spite of the fear you feel. Take courage, and lead anyway. God is with you.

A third wrong belief that traps many husbands is, "I'm not successful enough to lead." The husband might feel that, since he is just a stock boy at his job, he hasn't earned the right to lead in his family. That's a trick Satan plays on men to convince them to sit back passively in their families. He wants us to believe that only presidents and CEO's have the experience necessary to lead others. What nonsense! God hasn't made us all presidents, but He has appointed each of us to rule our home. Your role in business isn't tied to your role in your home. Sometimes the men who make the best husbands occupy the lowest positions in the company they work for.

I think men struggle with their manhood because they've bought into the world's system of power. The world says that you need to gain money and position to be a person of influence, that that's what qualifies you for leadership. God says that wealth and position have nothing to do with leadership. A leader is a servant to his followers; the one who sets the example, gives direction, and reveals integrity. God has called men to lead. We don't have to wait for any corporate approval before doing so. Take these lies and set them aside. You will never know it all, you will never have perfect confidence, and you will never have all the life-experiences to make you absolutely sure of every choice you make. No one does. Sometimes you'll be insecure, but so what? Every leader is insecure at times.

Keep in mind this truth: *You don't earn the right to be the leader of your home*. It's not a matter of merit, but one of ordination. God ordained it. He commanded you to lead. So you are either leading or you are disobeying God. You may have been a selfish kid when you got married, but the moment you said, "I do," you became a leader.

THE LACK OF LEADERSHIP

Not only are there wrong beliefs, but I see a number of wrong behaviors in many husbands. Like all behaviors, these, in one way or another, grow out of the wrong beliefs discussed above.

The number one problem that I see in perhaps 80 percent of marriages, is that the man is passive. He backs away from situations that require leadership. When the moment of truth arrives, he leaves.

Have you ever seen that happen? There is confusion, a decision needs to be made, and the man seems to disappear. There's a crisis, something hard to come to grips with, and the husband backs away from it. "I'll think about it," he might say as he slowly withdraws. Inside, he feels unsure about what to do, insecure about himself, and worried about his position. Instead of leading and giving direction, he just sits by passively. Meanwhile, his wife's frustration and anger build.

It's my contention that when the husband doesn't lead, he sins. Passivity is a sin. If I don't rule my house, if I don't take charge as the man of the house, I am living outside the will of God for my family. I've seen too many men remain passive in the face of trouble, and it causes serious problems with their families.

Perhaps our culture has built up the John Wayne image as the ideal for men that "average" men feel like they can't live up to it. In the movies, the Duke always knew what to do. He always made the right choices. He could do the brave thing, he could lick the bad guys, and he usually got the most beautiful girl at the end. But life is only like that in the movies. In real life, we often don't know what to do, we're afraid of getting whipped by the bad guys, and the beautiful girls never paid attention to us! This macho image has led to a bunch of men who are relationally disconnected, afraid of revealing their insecurities or allowing for failure. The only safe route left is to be passive and hope that somebody else bails us out of the situation or that things will turn out all right by themselves. Unfortunately, we often leave all that responsibility to our wives, and they aren't supposed to be doing our jobs for us anymore than anyone else is. Passivity is deadly for a Christian man who wants to be a First Chair father.

A man who remains passive for a long time develops a great deal of bitterness, anger, and unforgiveness in his life. He's mad at himself for being a wimp, but he'll store up his anger and attack his wife, accusing her of *keeping* him from being a man. This might sound irrational, but it goes on all the time. God put the desire to lead in man's heart, so a man who has been passive for years keeps a growing frustration inside. He'll direct his problem at the woman he thinks has somehow hindered him from becoming the man he wants to be. He chooses to forget that *he* is the one who has been sitting down, and she has simply stepped into a vacancy that needs to be filled.

This stored up rage can turn into verbal attacks and criticism. He speaks harsh words, and emotional abuse begins. Instead of being the leader, the husband becomes the bully. While at first he was passive, he is now abusive. And physical abuse of wives has become an epidemic in our society, largely because men have refused to lead the way God commanded them to in Scripture. They come up with their own ways of filling the need to lead.

If the man starts out as passive and then becomes abusive, the next step is usually absence. Having already abdicated his role as leader, the husband abdicates his role as father. He stays at the office later in the evening, spends more time with his buddies on the golf course, or disappears into the garage at night. "I don't want to deal with this," he says to himself, so he finds other ways to spend his time and energy, hoping those'll compensate for an unhappy home life.

I'm not describing only a few homes led by non-Christian men. This is a pattern I see played out again and again in our churches. The family looks fine on Sunday, showing up for church and Sunday school. But the relationship between husband and wife is dying, and the dynamics of the family are not at all what God intended.

The children who grow up under this kind of father never get a clear picture of God's plan for families. The Christian father who sits in the Second Chair has nothing to share with his children about the dynamics of the spiritual life. He can't point to his marriage as an example of how Christ loves the church and gave Himself for her. He can't reveal the awesome power of forgiveness and reconciliation that God offers through His Son Jesus Christ. So the kids, seeing that there is no power in Christianity, turn from it to seek other, happier answers.

WHAT IS A LEADER?

What picture comes to mind when you hear the word "leader"? Different people see leadership in different ways. Some people think it means great strength. Others see it as having great tenderness. Some people think it means a person who allows no discussion. Others see it as having a sort of collegial sharing. When it comes to leading your family from the First Chair, there are five key elements of leadership. As I talk with Christian wives across the country, these same principles come up again and again.

To begin with, as a First Chair leader *you are the protector of your family*. In a very real sense, your wife is the "damsel in distress" and you're the "knight in shining armor." As the leader, you are to keep her secure and safe. She should never have to go to bed worried or upset or fearful. Let your children know that you love them enough to die for them if need be. They are told in church that God is our heavenly Father; let them see how much an earthly father loves them, and they'll find it easier to trust the one in heaven.

I travel quite a bit, and whenever I come home, I can see my wife relax. It's like there's a big exhale, for her protector is home. Husband, to lead from the First Chair means you will protect your wife in the same way Christ protects the church. Don't let her have cause to worry about things—take care of them for her. Protect her from criticism, from danger, and from anxiety. You're the leader; it's your job. Even though you may not feel any more secure than your wife, take courage in the Lord. Be her protector.

Second, as a First Chair leader *you are the provider for your family*. You need to be the breadwinner so your wife doesn't have to worry about having enough money to pay the bills and put food on the table. Too many men stop being the provider and their wives have had to take jobs to help provide for their families. I know this is a touchy subject, but it's only touchy because Christians have accepted the world's lifestyle standards for their own. If the husband is the provider, you may have to live a simpler lifestyle.

When you first hear that, both you and your wife may complain, "But we *like* our lifestyle!" There's no question that it's great to live in a beautiful house, own new cars, and wear the best fashions. But keep in mind that those are the standards the world has set. Would you be willing to give up some of that if it would mean a more satisfying marriage relationship? Would you be willing to compromise on some worldly material goods if that meant significant improvement in your children's spiritual life? The husband who says, "You need to get a job so we can buy another car," admits that he values a car more than he values fulfilling God's plan.

Please don't misunderstand me; I'm not saying that a wife should never work outside the home. There are times when she may choose to work for one reason or another. But if the husband is the provider, she doesn't *have* to work to pay the bills. The pressure is off. She can fulfill her role as wife, she has the time to nurture her children from the First Chair, and she doesn't have the anxiety that comes with having to work to make ends meet. Too many Christian families are caught in the trap of materialism. By simplifying your lifestyle, you set a First Chair example to your children that some things are more important than money.

I know that there are some single mothers reading this, and my heart goes out to you. You may have no choice in the matter; you must work to provide for your family. That's a difficult situation, and one that the modern church isn't doing enough to alleviate. In the early church, if a husband died, the church family helped the mother raise her children. Men in the church would take the time to talk with the kids, so that they grew up knowing what a First Chair man was like. But today, with the time demands we put on people and the rise in divorces that are rampant both inside and outside the church, the Body rarely offers effective assistance to single mothers.

A third principle of leadership for First Chair fathers is that *you are the point man for your family.* The point man is like a scout on a wagon train. When the wagons get lost in the wilderness, the scout says, "Wait a minute, I know the way to go." Then he points out the right direction for everyone to follow. When your family sees you sitting in the First Chair, communicating with God and obeying His commands, they'll develop a new appreciation for God's leading in their lives.

My father was like a scout. When I was very young, the doctor told my parents that my sister would die of asthma if we didn't move to another climate. Now, my folks had six children, and we didn't come from a wealthy family, so moving all the way across the country wasn't an easy thing to do. Yet my dad packed up the family and set out for a new home. Years later I asked my father what it was like.

"Did you have a job?"

"No," he replied.

"Did you have much money saved?"

"Hardly any," he admitted.

"What did you do?"

"I said to your mom, 'Sweetheart, our daughter's in trouble. It's time to move.'"

Now *that's* a point man. He just said, "Don't worry, we'll find a way," and he moved. I think that, deep inside, most men want to be the point men. They want to point the way for their families. (Maybe that's why they never want to look at maps or ask directions when they're lost!) And the fact is, most women I've interviewed feel good about their husband being that because they long to be led and that's part of leadership. When there's a crisis at your house, and everything is falling apart in mass confusion, the point man will say, "Attention everyone! We're going this way. Pack your bags." You see, somebody has to make the final decision in a family. Of course, you should talk it over. A wise leader gets as much information as possible; he doesn't jump on the first alternative offered. But when there's a confusing mess as to what the family should do, the First Chair father leads. He might say, "We're going to do it my way," or it might be, "OK, we'll go your way." But he *never* says, "I don't want to talk about it. You decide." That's not leading! A First Chair father serves as point man, offering godly direction to his family.

A fourth principle of First Chair leadership is that *you are the priest of your family*. The priest was God's representative to His people, serving as the spiritual leader and setting an example of godliness and service to everyone. Husbands, take your families to church. Make sure they get spiritual food. Pray with your wife and your children. Encourage them and make sure they are growing in the Lord. Too many Christian men allow their wives to be the spiritual leader in the home. That's a mistake. Let your kids see that you have a close relationship with God, and that your earnest desire is for them to experience the same.

The priest was also there to minister to those in need. When your wife is hurting, be there for her. When your children experience broken hearts, mend them. When they need a word of encouragement, nourish them. Let them know that you are there to serve, and they'll see how a First Chair Christian treats others. Sometimes we need to help our wives cry out. Sometimes we need to tell them to go to bed and relax. You take the kids, you clean the house, you do the dishes, you make dinner, and she stays in bed to read. As the minister, you want to make sure your wife feels nourished, cared for, and strengthened. A leader isn't all bluster and commands. He is also a tender, caring servant.

Finally, the fifth principle of First Chair leadership is that *you are the prince of your family*. Christ is King, and you, a brother of the King's, are His representative to your family. You're the prince. There is nobility, dignity, and integrity inherent in royalty. There is honor in being a prince, but it is an honor steeped in humility, for you were not born a prince. God made you a prince when you became part of His family. It wasn't your work that brought this royalty, it was all God's doing. So you treat the members of your family with tender care. You reveal to them the dignity that comes with being God's representative. You keep your word to your wife, and show your sons and daughters how a man of integrity lives. You do what's noble, even if it means you don't get to do everything you want to do.

One of the things that has impressed me about royal families is their sense of duty. I read a story recently about the Queen of England, who was traveling to New Guinea to visit some of the former domain of Great Britain. It is imperative for the Queen to eat whatever the nationals consider a delicacy, so as to not offend anyone. During a stop in Papua, the Queen was offered bat wing soup. Now, I don't know if I could have beared to *look* at it, let alone eat it, but the Queen smiled and spooned it down. And the story reveals that this sort of thing is common when royalty visit primitive cultures. Imagine the graciousness and tact it would take to survive the food and not offend the populace! The Queen has a duty to her heritage. So, too, every husband has a duty to lead and care for his family with grace and patience.

I think every man, down deep, wants to be the prince of his family. His home is his castle, and his wife his queen. All hell can break loose outside the walls, but inside the prince keeps everyone safe. Even if he loses his job, the husband is the prince at home. His monetary status has nothing to do with his nobility. As a prince, he offers his family a picture of the grace of God.

ASPIRE TO LEAD

Our world has completely misread the issue of family leadership. The cry of "equality!" has gone up from the feminist movement, suggesting it is somehow wrong for men to desire to lead. But Scripture speaks clearly of the man being the head of the family, even though he is equal to his wife in the sight of God. First Timothy Chapter 3 says, "Here is a trustworthy saying: If a man sets his heart on being an overseer, he desires a noble task" (v. 1). So you see, it is a good thing for a man in the church to want to be a leader. However, note that one of the qualifications for leadership is that he "must rule his own house well, having his children in submission with all reverence. For if a man does now know how to rule his own house, how will he take care of the church of God?" (vs. 4-5).

The man should rule his house, but he should rule it well. If he can't lead his small family at home, he certainly can't lead God's larger family at church. Leading at home is God's preparation to leading at church. The First Chair father makes sure he reveals his spiritual life to his own family before he displays it to the entire church. And as his children see that his faith is sincere, and that God has done a work in their father's life, they will not only desire a First Chair relationship with God, but they will honor their father publicly.

It's sad to see the children of Christians turning to rebellion, but that's what happens when they discover the faith of their father is not sincere. They can't respect someone whom they see as being a phony. However, if they see that their father is honest about his faith, and they see God move in his life, they'll respect him in private and in public. I once watched the ordination of a middle-aged man, whose son said publicly, "My father is the most godly man I know. When I look at him, I see how Jesus Christ must have been." What an honor to have your children hold you in such high regard.

Jesus told a story of a king who returned from a trip. He gathered his servants together and asked them to give an accounting of their lives.

"What did you do while I was away?" the king asked his servants. Each offered his own story. One servant had been obedient, and he received a reward for being a good and faithful man. "You have been faithful in little, you shall be put in charge of much."

Sometimes, I don't think people quite understand what that parable is all about. Christ Himself is the King, and He will return one day to get an accounting from His servants. He will return to rule over this world, and those who have proven themselves faithful will rule with Him. That is why leadership is one of the most significant of spiritual exercises. Perhaps how you rule your home will determine how much Christ gives you to rule on this earth when He returns. Lead your family from the First Chair, and they will love you forever. Lead your family from the First Chair, and the Lord may reward you with leadership forever.

THE FIRST CHAIR HUSBAND

Imagine a telephone conversation that goes like this: "Hi, honey, how's your day at office going? Oh...well I made a reservation for seven. What time will you be home?...But we had plans!...Oh. Well, no, that's all right. It's just that we haven't had a night out in a while and I thought...O.K. Yeah, sure, it's okay. Bye."

The wife hangs up, and she's thinking, "Something has come up—for the third time this month? Maybe he just doesn't want to be with me. Maybe I'm too old...or too dull. He used to send me flowers for no reason at all. He noticed everything—new dress, new haircut. Now he comes home, sits down, flips on the TV, and doesn't even seem to see me. I wonder if I'm enough for him any more. I wonder why I don't feel loved...."

Sound familiar? Too many couples start sounding that way after a while. Consider this: What impact does that sort of relationship have on your children? What are they thinking when they see their parents take each other for granted? What impact can the love of a First Chair husband toward his wife have on his children?

THE LOVING LEADER

You remember when you first fell in love with your mate. You couldn't take your eyes off her, or write her enough poems, or buy her enough candy. The rest of the world was irrelevant, as long as you could spend time with your soul-mate. You showered all the love humanly possible onto her, because she's the one you loved above all else. If anyone had asked you, "What will you do when you fall out of love?" you'd have thrown something at him. No engaged person wants to believe he'll ever have a problem loving his spouse. But it happens to all of us. I don't know if there is a couple alive who never thought to themselves, "You don't love me anymore."

Maybe that's why the New Testament clearly reveals the commands of the Lord to couples. God didn't want there to be any ambiguity at all. "Husbands, *love your wives just as Christ loved the church and gave Himself up for her*" (Ephesians 5:25). Sure, God tells the man to be the leader, but He doesn't want you to be an autocratic, domineering, abusive leader. He wants you to be a loving leader.

How did Christ love the church? That passage in Ephesians Chapter 5 goes on to say that Jesus "gave Himself up for her to make her holy, cleansing her by the washing with water through the word, and to present her to Himself as a radiant church, without stain or wrinkle or any other blemish, but holy and blameless. In this same way, husbands ought to love their wives as their own bodies. He who loves his wife loves himself. After all, no one ever hated his own body, but feeds and cares for it, just as Christ does the church" (Ephesians 5:26-29).

Christ presents a beautiful picture of what pure love is. He gave Himself. Rather than thinking of his own interests, He thought of the interests of His bride. That's why Christ was willing to die for the church. Though painful, it was in the best interest of the church in the long run. He did everything possible to protect her and keep her clean. He fed and cared for her. He loved his bride, the church, better than His own body. What a loving leader!

This passage is usually used to describe how a husband ought to love his wife, using Christ and the church as an example. However, it can just as easily be used to describe Christ's relationship to His church using God's plan for marriage as an example. The two relationships are to mirror one another. Caring, loving, protecting, and giving sacrificially for another's best interests are the hallmarks of Christ, and they are to be the hallmarks of a marriage relationship.

There aren't many strong marriages in this world for your kids to see. There aren't many strong marriages in the church for your kids to see. If their future wedded life is shaped by what they see in the movies and on TV, their lives will be filled with cutting comments, extramarital affairs, and sexual disappointment when they discover that making love isn't always the earth-shaking experience played out on the silver screen. Instead, expose them to *your* strong marriage, and give them a model to follow. As you sit in the First Chair, let them see not only how you long to be like Jesus, but how you want to treat others like Jesus did. This First Chair experience is crucial to their future relationships. When Darlene and I worked with young people, our home was regularly filled with kids who wanted to hang around us just to see our marriage. I think many of them saw nothing terribly exciting about their parent's marriage, so they came over just to watch two people who demonstrated their love to each other on a regular basis.

Our world is filled with hurting, broken relationships. Much of the sexual revolution of our generation occurred because people were trying to find meaning through their relationships with others. Fathers, it's your job to help your children see that strong, fulfilling marriages can happen, but only if you love with Christ's love. You show them that by demonstrating your deep love to your wife on a regular basis. That allows your sons to observe how a godly man treats a woman, so that he has a healthy pattern to follow as he grows up. It allows your daughters to see how a Christian woman should be treated, and she can quickly dump the joker who treats her like she is his plaything!

Children who don't see love demonstrated at home have no pattern to follow. They enter marriage without a model. Kids who don't know for certain that Dad loves Mom feel uncertain, and often rebel at the perceived shallowness of their parent's relationship. Dad, you aren't just called to lead. You are called to lead in a particular way. You are to be the loving leader in your home.

THE SECRET OF LOVE

Why does love start to be a problem after several years of marriage? Why do we go from hearing sweet nothings to hearing sour naggings? You used to want to paint the town with your favorite girl, and now you find yourself just painting the kitchen every three years. You used to bring her flowers, now you pull the weeds. What's the secret to staying in love?

I found a quote from Chuck Swindoll that sums up the secret to maintaining your love:

> "Love is the one business in which it pays to be absolutely lavish. To give it away, throw it away, splash it all over, empty your pockets, shake the baskets...and tomorrow, you'll have more than ever."

That's wonderful. If you lavish love on your spouse, you'll have more than ever. But if you hold back, because you think your mate is holding back, love will shrink and die. David Mace said, "One of the greatest illusions of our time is that love is self-sustaining; that once you fall in love, you'll stay in love. It's not true. Love must be fed and nurtured and constantly renewed. Love in the heart wasn't put there to stay; love isn't love 'til you give it away."

When Paul tells husbands to "love" their wives, he uses the Greek word *agapo,* which is the same word Christ used to tell us that "God so *loved* the world." It's an imperative word—a command, if you will. It's something you choose to do or not do. The choice is yours. You can obey or disobey. You can *choose* to love your wife, or choose to not love her. Agape love doesn't keep going by itself, it's a choice you make to love. So if you feel like you don't love your wife anymore, you can change your feelings by simply choosing to do so. Choose to love her. Decide that you will do so.

I once counseled a man who hated a member of his family. He had nurtured that hate for twenty years. It was vicious, and it was fresh. When I asked him, "How on earth can you keep a hate alive for so long?" He told me, "I keep it there every day."

You see, you can choose to hate, or you can choose to love. You can simply decide that you are going to obey God's command and love your wife. We talk about love as an emotion in our culture, and some in the church have tried to deny that. "No," they say, "love isn't an emotion. It's an action." I think that neglects the obvious fact that love is a very emotional thing. Love has actions that flow from it, but it is an emotion, and it does us no good to deny the fact. When Scripture tells you to love your wife, it doesn't simply mean to do nice things for her. It means to love her; passionately, fervently, and with great emotion. And I believe that once a man makes up his mind to love his wife, repents of his sin and declares his intention to obey God, the emotion arrives. I've seen couples who hated each other so much they wouldn't even speak, but when they repent and commit to loving each other, they suddenly find themselves filled with an emotional love. My wife and I have gone through times when we've been angry and aching, unloving toward one another, then suddenly something happens and we fall into each other's arms, filled with the emotion of love.

You *are* in control of your emotions. Your heart may be hard and disobedient so that you choose not to feel anything, but all you have to do is make the choice to show love and the emotion arrives. When Christ spoke to the church at Ephesus in Revelation Chapter 2, He warned the believers that they had "fallen away from your first love." That is, they were no longer in love with God. They were going through the motions, but their hearts weren't in it. What was the solution?

"Remember the height from which you have fallen! Repent, and do the things you did at first" (Revelation 2:5).

That's the secret of loving.

Do you remember how you used to act when you were head over heels in love with your wife? Start doing those things again. Call her on the phone and tell her how much you love her. Surprise her with flowers. Take her to dinner. Go on a walk with her. Send her a love note telling her how beautiful she is. Do the things you did at first, and the love will return.

Imagine the impact on a child who sees love demonstrated by his father to his mother. He sees Dad treat Mom with respect. He sees Dad protect her from worry. He sees Dad treat her with kindness. And that child begins to understand how Christ loves the church. He starts to see what love is like, and how it differs from the lust that is paraded on the television. He sees what sort of man he can be if he will sit in the First Chair, and that changes him. Your daughter begins to see what sort of relationship she can have if she'll reside in the First Chair, and she'll settle for nothing else.

On the other hand, a child who doesn't see love demonstrated begins to seek the love he or she craves elsewhere. He will go outside the family to get it, thinking that his parents don't have love to give away. Many become involved in sexual relationships in the hope of finding the love they desire. The love Dad displays in the home can impact his children for the rest of their lives.

LOVE IN ACTION

A woman who is shown sacrificial love has no chance—*she has to love in return*. There's no getting away from it. I've seen countless women nod their heads in agreement. No woman alive can rebuff sacrificial love. They blossom under it. On the other hand, every time I've counseled a couple in which the wife has had an affair, after digging through all the dirt we eventually come to the start of the problem: "I didn't feel loved anymore by my husband."

When Paul tells husbands to love their wives, he doesn't mean to love them once. The word is in the active voice, which means you are to continually love her. Don't stop actively choosing to love your wife. She's got to see your love demonstrated regularly. Not once a month on a date. Not once a week when you want to make love. All the time.

I asked my mom, "What did you say to Dad when he said you were moving across the country? He had no job, little money, six kids—and he wanted to drag you across the continent to a place where you didn't know a soul?"

My mom started laughing. "Bruce, we were in love! I told him, let's go!"

That sums up what sort of impact a loving leader can have. When you love your wife, she responds to your love. She sees that you are picking her above all others. You're holding her up, admiring her, lavishing warmth and caring upon her, celebrating her very existence.

Christ loved the church by giving it exactly what it needed. It needed a Savior, and a way to God that could take the penalty for all our sins. So Christ died for us, at a serious personal loss. Of course, the church has at times not responded properly to that love; we haven't always been loving in return. But Christ still loves us unconditionally. Even when we fail, He continues to love.

The First Chair husband shows his children what unconditional love means by loving his wife at all times. He appreciates the love and mercy God has shown him so much that he is willing to show it to others. Now, he won't be perfect. None of us sit in the First Chair all the time. But he makes that effort to always reveal his love for his wife, and he makes sure his kids see him make the effort. It's easy to love someone when they are treating you kindly, but unconditional love is displayed when you love someone even in the face of anger or neglect. The good news is that that kind of loving will eventually bring about the desired response in your mate.

LOVING AS YOU LOVE YOURSELF

Most people who see a counselor don't need mental help nearly as much as they need someone to love them. Paul Tournier has said, "I am convinced that nine out of ten persons seeing a psychiatrist do not need one. They need somebody who will love them with God's love and they will get well."

We hear many modern psychologists say that lack of self-esteem is a major problem these days. I disagree. I think the biggest problem is too much self-love. Nobody really hates themselves; they simply have too much self-love. I have yet to find a man who is happy, satisfied with his life, and not in love with his wife. A man not in love with his partner is profoundly sad. His attitude might be, "I don't care about you. I'll live my own life and be happy." But he never is because, according to Scripture, the two are one. If you hurt her, you end up hurting yourself. If you toss barbs at her, you'll feel it in the end. When you don't love her, you hurt yourself.

If you really want to love her as you love yourself, answer this question: What would you enjoy? Well, if you want to bring pleasure to your wife, do the things that bring her pleasure. Surprise her with a night out. Bring some romance into your relationship. Take her out to dinner and hold her hand across the table, the way you used to when you were engaged.

Not long ago I took my daughter to lunch. There was an engaged couple at the next table, totally oblivious to the world. They held hands across the table. She stared deeply into his eyes. They didn't say much. Suddenly she had tears in her eyes. I could see she wasn't upset, just filled to the brim with love for her knight in shining armor. He took out his hankie, reached across the table, and dabbed the corners of her eyes. Suddenly my daughter said, "Oh, Dad...that's beautiful!" And it was. Then she said, "It reminds me of you and Mom."

My daughter was struck with the couple's love after seeing it just once. Imagine the impact you can have on your kids by displaying that sort of love to your wife on a regular basis. This is another way you can ask your children to climb into your lap as you sit in that First Chair, and say, "Watch. This is how Christ loved the church. See what great love! You can experience that love."

Saint Augustine once said, "One loving heart sets another on fire." Your love for your wife can fan her love into flame, and it can kindle a fire in the hearts of your children as they see you love her. Strike the match, gentlemen. Love your wives.

1. How can a father show his children that he has first-hand faith?

2. What does it mean to be the *head* of a household?

3. What is your definition of Christian leadership?

4. Who has the strongest marriage you've ever seen? What makes it so strong?

5. What three things could you do to strengthen your wife?

CHAPTER TWELVE

The First-Chair Mother

American culture wants women to believe that they've been stepped on for a long time, prevented from achieving their personal goals, and treated like doormats by men. You know what? It's right. Too many men have not viewed women from God's perspective—as valuable, important partners, equal in the sight of God. Unfortunately, the solution offered by the feminist movement is equally as bad. They want to punish men, push women into careers, and do away with all differences between the sexes. Those answers range from wrong-headed to downright absurd. God made man and woman different, and to deny the differences is to deny the truth. Our bodies are different, our temperaments are different, and our roles are different. Why would we want to make everyone the same? When the world was all one sex, God looked at it and said it was "not good."

A woman is not a doormat. She is a unique creation of the Almighty God, made specially to be a "suitable helper," according to Genesis Chapter 2. A good understanding of the woman's role as helper will clear up many of the misconceptions about women and put you on track toward using your position in the First Chair to impact your children.

WHAT IS A MOM?

Who on earth does a woman ask to find out about being a mother? The culture? Women's magazines and daytime talk shows are filled with suggestions on becoming the perfect woman. Their answers, though, don't always seem to connect with reality, and there seem to be a surprising number of divorced women doing the talking. Does a woman look to the church? Friends in Sunday school may have some ideas, but too often the ones doing the most talking are the last ones you'd turn to for advice. Does she turn to family? She might, but many women don't know who to ask, or who to trust, when it comes to sensitive issues about being a wife and mother. Of course, she can always turn to the Bible, but she might not be willing to, since society has told us those male-dominated Scriptures are just old fashioned, sexist polemics aimed at keeping men in charge. So who does she listen to?

The source to which you turn for an answer will determine what you believe. Over time, the concept of truth changes in society, and in ours it has come to the point that many people today no longer believe there is such a thing as "absolute truth." The concept of truth changes among Second Chair people at churches, who always feel a need to compromise between God's standards and those of the world. But the one source we can go to for solid, unchanging truth is the Word of God. So put your presuppositions aside for a moment and let's take a look at what God has to say about being a mom.

"And the Lord God said, 'It is not good for the man to be alone. I will make a helper suitable for him" (Genesis 2:18). I find it remarkable that God said something He had put into place was "not good." Creation was incomplete without woman. God had created a man to tend the garden, but He wasn't done with creation yet. So—watch this carefully—God created a *helper*. Many people believe that the Lord created a companion, to keep Adam from being lonely. But that's not what the text says. Adam needed more than somebody to talk to. He needed a helper to accomplish something. So what God did was to create exactly what Adam needed.

That word translated "helper" was commonly used in the Hebrew language to denote an assistant. That's what a wife is to her husband—a helper. That's what a mother is to her children—a helper. She is a nurturer. She is someone who helps accomplish the task *which the man could never do by himself.* Men, you can say good-bye to the idea that you're a rock, someone who doesn't need anybody else. You need your wife. You're incomplete without her. And your wife isn't just any old helper, but a helper "suitable" for you, according to Genesis. She isn't a slave, but a special creation, equal in the sight of God, but with the unique role of supporting you rather than leading you.

The woman is also the helper to the children. In Genesis Chapter 1, God told Adam and Eve to "be fruitful and increase in number; fill the earth and subdue it. Rule over the fish of the sea and the birds of the air and over every living creature that moves on the ground" (Genesis 1:28). That's the commission God gave to the very first couple. Notice that they were both called to the same mission, but they were to do it in tandem: one is the head and the other is the helper. They were to have kids (which neither could do on his own) and they were to subdue the earth (which neither could do on his own). Man cannot complete the world-wide task of filling or subduing the earth without woman. As man is responsible to be the leader and say, "Let's accomplish this," the woman is responsible to come along and say, "I'm here to help."

This is anathema to the modern feminist, who believes a separate career is necessary to make a woman's life fulfilling. But this isn't demeaning to women; indeed nothing is more exalting than to complete the perfect plan God has designed for her. Mothers, think about the influence you have on your daughters. They are going to be inundated with messages from the world about how they need to find careers, and what a hindrance children are, and why they must break free from the shackles of our male-dominated society. What difference would it make if they were to watch you enjoy your role as helper? What influence could you have on your children by revealing to them your love for God and for your husband? If they see you in the First Chair, fulfilled in obeying God's designed role for you, what lasting impact will that make in their lives?

That's an important question for you to consider. A mother who glories in the role God created, rather than trying to impress the world by fulfilling society's expectations, can make a great impression on her kids. She can reveal to her sons the importance of loving God enough to obey. She can display to her daughters the completeness found only in God's plan for marriage. And as she remains close to the Lord, her children will see how a person who loves God behaves, offering a First Chair experience to those who need it most.

THE COUNTERPART

Your children need to know how moms and dads differ. Not just how they are different physically, but how they are different emotionally and personally. Most babies form a bond with their mothers that their fathers could never provide. The closeness, nourishment, and nurturing offered by the mother is exactly what a baby needs. I used to marvel at the relationship Darlene had with the kids, and I knew that somehow I would never experience that. Her relationship with them was unique, just as I would have a unique father's relationship to them as they got older.

The Bible says that the woman God created was "suitable" for Adam. I love that word. It can also be translated "comparable" or "fitting," but literally it means "opposite." Isn't that interesting? Eve was the opposite of Adam, but in a positive way. In a way that brought out what he lacked. Eve was designed by God to fill in Adam's gaps. The best word in English is probably "counterpart." A counterpart is a person or thing that closely resembles another, but when added to the other somehow completes it. Adam was incomplete without his counterpart Eve. According to Genesis, God fashioned her to suit Adam.

Sure, men and women are opposites. You don't have to look very far to see plenty of evidence of that. People in our culture who want to deny that fact and turn us into a unisex society are fighting an impossible battle. They're warring with the plan of God. He brings those opposites together to create one flesh, and the two pieces fit perfectly. For someone to claim, "I'm married, but I've found a better partner than the one I now have," is totally false. God created your partner for you. How can you improve on the plan of God?

I overheard a grandmother at the supermarket say to her granddaughter, "Oh, I forgot to get the cocoa. Your grandpa loves his chocolate cake."

The granddaughter thought a minute and said, "Don't you get tired of cooking for him?"

"Heavens, no!" came the reply. "Sometimes I get tired of the work, but I never get tired of helping your grandpa. It makes him happy, and that makes me happy. Doesn't that make sense?"

As I stood by them, it was all I could do to keep from saying, "Yes, it does!" That's exactly the attitude a Christian wife should have. She is the loving counterpart to her husband, helping him whenever she can because that is her God-given role.

The feminist movement is nothing more than a worldly wail against God's plan. Its leadership seems to believe that no woman can be satisfied until she's on her own, separated from all men. But following selfish goals instead of God's plan never leads to happiness, and most of the hard-core feminist leaders are some of the most unhappy people I've ever seen. Their philosophy has led to an acceptance of abortion and lesbianism as social benefits, even though both are evil in the eyes of God. Abortion is, in my mind, the ultimate selfish act: taking the life of another because it is inconvenient for you. These ideas come from Satan, who is battling the ideas of God by substituting his own evil philosophy into our society.

Has feminism brought a better understanding to the sexes? No, it has separated them and created more animosity than ever. Has it brought more joy and fulfillment to marriages? No, it has led many women to divorce their husbands to go in search of some alternative happiness that doesn't exist. People who reject the plan of God can never be happy.

First Corinthians says, "I want you to realize that the head of every man is Christ, and the head of the woman is man, and the head of Christ is God....For man did not come from woman, but woman from man; neither was man created for woman, but woman for man....In the Lord, however, woman is not independent of man, nor is man independent of woman. For as woman came from man, so also man is born of woman. But everything comes from God" (1 Corinthians 11:3,8,9,11,12). You see, woman is the counterpart of man, the perfect complement. God designed a wife as a counterpart to her husband. As she sits in the First Chair, loving God and helping him, the children see what God intended a woman to be. They can makes sense of things with which most of the world still struggles.

HOW TO BE A HELPER

The man has a difficult task: he must lead, even if he doesn't feel qualified. The woman had a difficult task: she must help, even if she feels more qualified to lead than her husband. It's only when they work together, seeking the guidance of God and resting in the First Chair, that they become comfortable with their roles.

Since the Lord brought the woman to the man as a helper, the best words she can utter, to be totally obedient to God, are the words, "How can I help you?" There are many things a man might feel that he can't handle, and he would be lifted, enabled, and encouraged if his wife were to ask how to help. "What would you love for me to do? How can I help you reach your dream? What can I do to enable you to become the man you want to be?" Those are some of the most empowering words possible. They'll make a husband feel as though he's not alone, that he's got a team pulling for him to succeed. Every successful man I know, whether he be in business or farming or ministry, has a remarkable woman behind him. When he's down, she picks him up, whether she is down or not. When he loses his way, she tells him that she still believes in him. She has the role of helping her man reach God's dream for him.

This isn't easy, but then, what part of the Christian life is easy? It's difficult for any of us to make ourselves second, to play the part of a helper or a servant instead of a leader. Everything in our inner beings fight against it. A wife will *want* to lead. God said in Genesis 3:16 that her desire would be for her husband's place. But if she will take the role of helper, she'll soon find the fulfillment she could never find in a hard-driving career.

I think many wives are working hard, but not helping their husband, and that causes all sorts of problems in the family. The daughters see that behavior and believe that what's important are their own goals, not the goals of the partner. The sons see the behavior and begin to believe that men are on their own, totally alone in achieving their goals. The children see the lack of unity in the marriage, and begin to wonder if marriage shouldn't provide more closeness. They see parents going their own separate ways, and they long for a relationship in which the goals are shared. I believe that every person on earth wants to share his life. God calls some to be single, but even singles admit that is a hard row to hoe.

The mother is not only the helper of her husband; she is the helper of her children. As you look through Scripture, you'll find that all the fathers made some serious error in parenting: Abraham, Isaac, Jacob, and Solomon. It is hard to find an example of a godly father who's son also loved the Lord. But the Scripture is filled with examples of mothers who nurtured and cared for their children: Sarah, Rachel, Deborah, Mary, Naomi, Elizabeth, and Hannah are just a few examples.

The Jews have a wise saying: No country is greater than its mothers, for they are the makers of men. Hanna was a helping mother. In the first few chapters of 1 Samuel, you can find this godly woman praying for a child. Samson, the great leader of Israel, had died, leaving his nation in turmoil. There was a corrupt priest, a weak nation, and a spiritual decline among the Jews. God needed a spiritual man to guide Israel, so He looked for a spiritual mother to shape him. There are three things that stand out to me as I look at Hannah.

First, *she had a right relationship with her husband.* She worshipped with him, even though he wasn't perfect. She shared her affection with him, even though he was a polygamist. You can see the grace, forgiveness, and love that this woman had for her husband. That love was expressed in her worship of God.

Second, *she had a right relationship with God*. Hannah wept in prayer to God because she didn't have a son. But she still kept faith in Him. She had a passion for God's best, and she promised the Lord she would give her son back to Him if God would only give her a child. She remained close to the Lord, spending considerable time in prayer. Not only was she a woman of prayer and purity, she was a woman of patience, waiting for God to answer her prayer. The result of her faith was the birth of Samuel, whose name means "heard by God." Hannah wanted God's best, and the Lord responded to her faithfulness.

Third, *she had a right relationship at home*. Hannah knew her priorities. She weaned her son, then surrendered him to the Lord as she had promised. She made sure Samuel had the training, love, and care he needed to grow in the Lord. Her husband agreed with her decision, and it created even more harmony in their home. Although Hannah gave up her son Samuel, the Scriptures say she was blessed with seven more children. And she was able to see Samuel become one of the greatest priests Israel ever had.

A mother who sits in the First Chair can have the same sort of influence on her children. She can reveal her faith to them, keep a right relationship with God and let them see her devotion to Him. She can allow them to see her praying and reading her Bible. She can help her children understand the stories of Scripture. And she can make sure they see her as the helper. That will help them see what God intended the roles of husbands and wives to be, and they won't grow up with the confused values of the world, seeking love in relationships that don't last. Rather than battling for leadership in the home, she can help her husband succeed at being the man God desires him to be. The children, then, will sense the harmony and want what you have.

During one great battle, Moses had to keep his arms up in the air to gain victory. Any time he let them down, the armies of Israel began to lose. Eventually, others had to come and stand beside

Moses to help him keep his arms in the air. That succeeded, and Israel won the day. A woman can lift up the arms of her husband: that is a key factor in his winning life's battles. I would be lost without my wife—disabled, because she enables me; discouraged, because she encourages me; weak, because she empowers me.

A Christian mother can hold up the arms of her husband. When she helps him to succeed, his life and family will change.

FIRST CHAIR WIVES

There is a rule that is widely used in management circles called "The Twenty-Eighty Rule." It says that twenty percent of the things we do control eighty percent of the results. For example, twenty percent of the people in your church do eighty percent of the work. Twenty percent of the donors to your favorite ministry give eighty percent of the money. And twenty percent of the things you do in your life will bring about eighty percent of your success. Sometimes large results are found in little things.

I mention this because the rule can be applied to your marriage. In my view, eighty percent of your marital harmony and success will depend on one small factor: biblical submission. What is the importance God places on submission in marriage? In Colossians 3:18 we read, "Wives, submit to your husbands, as is fitting in the Lord." Ephesians 5:22 says, "Wives, submit to your husbands as to the Lord." Paul instructed Titus that wives are "to submit to their husbands" in Titus 2:5. Likewise 1 Peter 3:1 reads, "Wives, in the same way be submissive to your husbands...." The Lord makes this teaching a priority in Scripture, so before we toss it away we ought to at least see what Christ is calling wives to do, and how it can affect their children.

BIBLICAL SUBMISSION

The word "submit" seems almost to be a dirty word today, but it comes from a beautiful Greek word. It's actually a combination of two words: *upo*, which means to be under, and *tasso*, which means to arrange or organize. When you submit, you organize yourself underneath another person. When the Bible tells wives to submit, it is instructing them to arrange their lives under their husband's leadership. It's the same word the Centurion used when he told Jesus he was a man under authority. A soldier understands that his role is vitally important, but that there is an order which must be followed—a chain of command. So it is in God's plan for your family. Wives are under orders to submit.

If that sounds too strong, remember that the phrase is an imperative, just like the command "thou shall not kill." This is an instruction from God. For a wife to not submit is for her to live in disobedience. However, husbands need to know that the phrase is active. That is, the wife chooses to obey or disobey. She isn't passive to her husband's activity; the man can't *make* her submit. A man doesn't browbeat his wife into submission; she chooses to do it herself. She comes under his leadership by choice, and that can be an extremely difficult thing for some women. The good news is that the Bible promises, "Humble yourself under the mighty hand of God, and in due season, He will lift you up." No one else humbles you; you humble yourself.

A wife may not feel like submitting, but that's irrelevant to God. No one likes to submit to another. None of us like to humble ourselves. But humility and bowing down to God is an essential part of our salvation. And a wife's submission to her husband is an essential part of fulfilling God's plan for your family.

The responsibility to submit belongs to the wife. *There is no verse of Scripture that encourages a man to "make your wife submit."* To do so is impossible, like a crusader holding a knife to the throat of a pagan and asking if he's interested in becoming a Christian. The words might be right, but his heart will never be in it.

THE CHARACTER OF SUBMISSION

When you sit in the First Chair, you want to obey Him. Your desire is to please the Lord in all things, and to reveal your relationship with God to your children so that they will know and love Him, too. While the father is the spiritual leader in the family, I think most kids pick up more about their relationship with God from their mother. Perhaps that is because kids are so often emotionally tied to their mother. More likely it is because women are relational beings. While men think in terms of activities and actions, women define their lives by their relationships. Children who don't see an authentic, obedient relationship between their mother and her God will turn to other gods for an answer.

That said, wives must understand that little will influence their children more than to see submission take place in the home. Everything in culture will mitigate against it, which should tell you how important an issue this must be. If Satan is fighting so hard to oppose submission, it must be a strategic element of God's plan for the family!

Your kids will see the concept of submission denigrated on television. They will hear it scoffed at by teachers and those in the media. Friends will shake their heads at the old-fashioned concept of submission. But if your children can see biblical submission in practice, and see the impact it has on the marriage relationship, they will understand how God's system is immeasurably better than the world's system. Let me suggest to you four characteristics of submission that will become clear to them.

First, *wives don't submit to every man; they submit to their husbands.* Scripture calls a wife to submit to her husband, but it doesn't call her to be a doormat to all men. When she got married she became part of a system, and her role in that system is under the leadership of her husband. But the issue is not one of all women submitting to all men. That's not God's plan. We all have some people to whom we are in submission in some context: the president, the governor, your local elected officials, the police, the court system, your superiors at work, your pastor, and the elders of your church are a few that come to mind. But that sort of submission touches all of us, not just women. I'm a man, but I am called to be submissive to those in authority over me (see Romans 13 and 1 Peter 2). The Bible doesn't tell wives to be second-class citizens. In society they might be leaders. But in the home, they submit to their husbands.

Submission to authority is really one of the biggest problems we face today. Young people have not been taught respect for authority, and that has moved society away from order and toward anarchy. Lack of respect for authority has led to juvenile delinquency, increased struggles between generations, and a diminishing concern for the elderly, who were formerly considered the wisest and most experienced members of society. A daughter who doesn't see her mom submit to authority in the home will struggle with submission to every authority in life. A daughter who sees her mother lovingly submit to the caring leadership of a husband will be willing to follow that pattern as she grows up.

A second characteristic of submission is that *a woman pleases God*. Several passages tell us that wives are to submit "as is fitting to the Lord." It is proper for a wife to submit; it seems correct. Things fit together best when she does. Regardless of what society says, submission of a wife to her husband pleases God, and pleasing the Lord should be her top priority when she's in the First Chair.

Another characteristic is that *she mirrors the relationship of the church to Christ*. The church is to follow the leadership of Jesus Christ in all things, because He is its head. When the Lord instructed the early church to go and be witnesses, they went. When He challenged them to remain pure, they took steps to cleanse themselves. The healthy church today spends considerable time in prayer, seeking the guidance of Lord, so that it can minister in accordance to His will. It does so because the people know that as soon as it forgets about God, it will flounder. A church that turns its back on Jesus Christ is a doomed church, according to Revelation Chapters 2 and 3. In the same way, a wife is to follow the leadership of her husband, for "just as the church is subject to Christ, let wives be subject to their own husbands." Think about how carefully the church wants to follow the guidance of God. It will do anything the Lord instructs, because the people in the church know that success is found in following Him. That's how carefully a wife is to submit to her husband, so that the pieces will fit together and she can experience all the blessing God intends for her marriage.

Fourth, *the submissive wife submits even when it's hard.* I once joked with my wife by saying, "Darlene, you're just not submissive." She about fell off her chair in surprise, but then I quickly added, "We almost always agree, so you never get your submission tested." You know, the real test of submission comes when one wants to go north and another wants to head south. That's the point at which a wife will have to wrestle with her ambition. Obviously, a wife isn't supposed to rob a bank because her husband asks her to, but that sort of situation seems mighty rare. More common is simply a circumstance where he wants to do one thing and his wife wants to do another. And husbands, I'd love to remind you to go back and look at what we discussed earlier, how the loving leader doesn't always demand his way. Biblically, the wife is to submit to her husband. The moment she doesn't feel like submitting is her opportunity to show the Lord she's willing to follow His commands, come what may.

The more your children see you pleasing God and obeying His Word, the greater their appreciation for your faith will be. As they see you sitting in that First Chair, obeying Him even when you don't want to—when she doesn't want to submit and he doesn't want to lead—they will begin to trust Him to guide their own lives. Submission is a key characteristic for a wife in the First Chair.

THE CONDUCT OF SUBMISSION

After reading that, some ladies would think, "You don't know my husband. If you did, you'd know that it's crazy to submit to him."

That argument implies that submission is based upon the husband making the right decision. But let's face it: he's not always going to make the right decision! What happens if he makes a tragic mistake? What happens if he's unfair? What happens if he's a grump? This is often where this teaching gives way to compromise. The wife of a pagan husband wants to know, "What does the Bible tell me to do if my man is flat-out disobedient?"

This is one of the hardest teachings of Scripture for many. 1 Peter 3:1 says, "Wives, in the same way be submissive to your husbands so that, if any of them do not believe the word, they may be won over without talk by the behavior of their wives." Even if a husband is terribly disobedient to God, a wife must submit to his leadership. She mustn't attack him verbally. Instead, she must let her good conduct bring him back. Does that man know he is living in sin? Probably. Is the Holy Spirit working on him? Yes. And the Holy Spirit, who is working on the inside, doesn't need a nagging "helper" on the outside. What softens a hard man is a woman who knows everything about him but still loves him. She'll win him over by her conduct.

Many times when I've counseled couples, it's the wife who wants to walk with God and the husband who wants to act like a total jerk. She's been preaching at him and leaving Christian books under his pillow, putting tracts in his lunch box and verses on his mirror, and the guy is saying, "If I hear one more thing about God I'll scream!" This doesn't work. Wives must learn to trust God, live in submission to, and honor their husbands.

Many years ago I went through a really tough time. I'd come home, sit on the couch in front of the TV, and wouldn't even be a part of the family. I was in bad shape, and Darlene told me about it. Then one night, as I plopped onto the sofa, she brought me dinner on a tray, then quietly sat down beside me. She didn't say a word, just sat with me. The next night was the same story, except this time she prepared my favorite meal. She brought it on a tray with flower, and said, "I love you." And you know, I didn't have a chance. My wife understood Scripture. She is not responsible for my disobedience. She is responsible to obey what the Lord commands. God takes over the rest of the work. And her submission melted the heart of this man. Respect and admiration in the midst of disobedience will melt nearly any man.

There are some ladies who live in obedience to God, maybe for a very long time, who see no result. But I can't find a verse that says, "Submit for a while, but if it doesn't work with your pagan husband, you can stop." I know this is tough, but a wife is called to be faithful to God even if her husband is not. She isn't responsible for his disobedience. God will deal with his disobedience. What a wife needs to do is trust God for that part, and do her part consistently.

Peter speaks of the impact a wife's conduct can have on her husband when he says, "they may be won over without talk by the behavior of their wives, when they see the purity and reverence of your lives" (1 Peter 3:2). That can also be translated, "when they observe your chaste conduct, accompanied by fear." The word Peter uses is *phobia*, a word we still use today to describe a strong fear. In other words, when a husband sees that his wife really respects him, that she is not just gritting her teeth and submitting to him, he'll be won over.

Peter goes on to say, "Your beauty should not come from outward adornment, such as braided hair and the wearing of gold jewelry and fine clothes. Instead, it should be that of your inner self, the unfading beauty of a gentle and quiet spirit, which is of great worth in God's sight" (vv. 3-4). The inner quality of a godly wife is her gentleness, her femininity. Men are attracted to her noble character, which brings beauty to the inside, not just the outside. That's the part a man falls in love with. There's nothing wrong with being attractive, mind you, but a First Chair wife focuses her attention on building her inner beauty, the jewelry of her heart.

On several occasions I've had the honor of speaking at conventions with Joni Earikson Tada. She was in a tragic accident and broke her neck, making her unable to move except for a very little bit. But every time I've been around her, I notice what the men say. They all say how beautiful she is because they're attracted to her inner character. She is gentle and feminine, and that's what men find so attractive about a woman.

Inner beauty. That's what draws a man to a woman. Her submission to God and to her husband will help build an inner beauty.

SUBMISSION REVEALS RESPECT

A woman wants a man who will love her. Through thick and thin, good times and bad, she can count on her husband to love her. God made women with that desire. But a man wants respect. Even when he's not respectable. By submitting to him, a wife reveals her respect for him. She honors him, and that will increase his love for her.

Leadership must be respected. We respect God, for He is great. The Bible tells us many times to "fear the Lord." And the word it uses is also *phobia*. Slaves are told to fear their masters with that same word. They are to offer respect, honor, dignity. No master deserves it the way God does, but the Bible calls slaves to offers it just the same. In the same way, wives are called to be submissive to their husbands. To offer them respect, even when they are unreasonable. As a matter of fact, Peter tells us that God finds it commendable if we show respect to someone and are treated unfairly. "To this you were called, because Christ suffered for you, leaving you an example that you should follow in His steps" (1 Peter 2:21).

When Jesus was given a task to do that was harsh, totally unreasonable and unfair, what did He do? He gave Himself for us. He "committed no sin, and no deceit was found in his mouth. When they hurled their insults at Him, He did not retaliate; when He suffered, He made no threats. Instead, He entrusted Himself to Him who judges justly" (v. 23). In His moment of submission, Christ obeyed.

Again, this is a tough teaching. It's particularly tough when a wife realizes that she is right and her husband is wrong about a particular issue. However, God may be trying to teach him a particular character quality that He can teach no better way than to let him fail. For a wife to fail to submit is to stand in the way of God.

Submission requires much trust in a loving God. It's really an issue between a wife and God, not between a wife and her husband. When a wife submits, she is obeying God's plan for your marriage. She is also revealing her faith in the Lord.

If a wife refuses to submit and she forces her own way, she doesn't really gain anything. She doesn't gain love. She doesn't gain trust. She doesn't develop any more faith in God. If she really wants to experience God's best for her life, she will have to come to that decision where she submits to her husband. And as she does so, she'll find herself sitting in that First Chair. The children will offer her respect because she has the courage to respect someone else. She'll experience the best God has for her life—and for her husband's.

STUDY QUESTIONS

1. What expectations does our culture put on women? How have those expectations changed in your lifetime?

2. In your own words, what is the biblical role of a wife and mother?

3. What does it mean to be a "counterpart"?

4. Does submission mean that a woman is subservient to a man?

5. What three things could you do to be a better helper?

CHAPTER THIRTEEN

Next Generation Thinking

You want your children to grow up loving God. You want them to sit in the First Chair. The best way to do that is to have a solid marriage. Experts tell us that the most common contributing factors to juvenile delinquency and rebellion in children are the lack of a father in the home, the lack of harmony in the home, a perceived lack of love, and the lack of discipline. If the dad is at least *in* your home, you've already got part of the problem licked. But if you work on improving your marriage relationship, you move toward achieving what I consider to be the single most important factor in raising godly kids. Your marriage can accomplish great things in the lives of your children.

I've known couples who have experienced difficult times with their kids but who have seen a dramatic turnaround in their homes because of the improvement in their relationships. An unhappy marriage makes a child feel insecure. Couples who are fighting often don't have the emotional energy needed to invest in their children. The kids get upset often, become familiar with tension and quarreling, and will sometimes act out in class to get attention from someone. Even negative attention is better than none at all to a love-starved child. Some children will become terribly shy, afraid to share with anyone what's happening at home.

Anger will build up in a youngster living in a house full of fighting. That anger can be expressed in kids through fighting, critical comments, sulleness, or acting up. When the child becomes a teenager, he or she can rebel against everything the parents believe. Their thinking is, "If my folks believe this and are so unhappy, why would I want to pattern my life after theirs?"

Building your marriage so that it conforms to the plan of God is essential in raising good kids. It will help them know what God intends, and is the best way of helping them to experience the love of God. Of course, you don't want to have kids who simply obey the rules. You desire children who sit in the First Chair, experiencing for themselves a close relationship with Jesus Christ. To do that, you have to think through a plan for nurturing their spiritual lives.

THE SPIRITUAL NEEDS OF YOUR FAMILY

Every child has some spiritual questions that need to be answered, some spiritual needs that must be met. As I watched my children grow up, I tried to be aware of what their needs were, so that at the appropriate time Darlene and I could introduce the spiritual truth that would meet that need. When one of our kids struggled with lying, we'd spend time talking about the importance of telling the truth. If our son was afraid, we'd talk about courage in the Lord. Some parents seem to think that telling a few Bible stories and taking their kids to Sunday school is enough to grow mature believers. It's not. You have to be looking for the times your children are most ready to receive spiritual teaching, and you have to have a plan in place that will help them grow. In my view, there are four significant needs that every child has.

First, *every child needs to know they are loved by God.* No one can have a First Chair experience unless he feels that God loves him. Love is a primary need for every human being. We are created with an innate longing for it. It's possible for men and women to spend their entire lives searching for love if they never experienced it as a child. I've known adults who have been in one reckless relationship after another in search of love, and I have known of many young people who broke their parents' hearts in a desperate search for love. If you want to meet your child's need for love, show them care when they are young. Cuddle them, touch them, and tell them they are loved. Even as they get older, never lose the ability to say, "I love you." Children who know they are loved at home can readily accept that they are loved by God, but kids who don't feel any love from home will have a very difficult time believing in a just and merciful God who loves them enough to die for them.

At a parenting conference, a woman who asked a question about this was encouraged to tell her rebellious son that she loved him. "Oh, I could never do that," she replied with a shake of her head. "We've never said that in our home." I was stunned. How can a parent watch a child grow and change, go through the ups and downs of childhood, and never say, "I love you"? Without those simple words, a child lives with insecurity. But a child who knows he is loved doesn't need to "look for love in all the wrong places," as the song says. He just has to look around him, and he knows there is love.

When you love your child, you embody God's love and concern for her. She can grow up believing in a loving heavenly father because she has had a loving earthly father. In one sense she has already experienced the love of being in the First Chair, for she has sat in her father's lap in his favorite chair.

Second, *every child has a spiritual need for direction*. One of the things that characterizes people in the Third Chair is their lack of direction. Having come to a belief that God doesn't work, they look for guidance and truth in other places. They might look at other religions, or they may turn their back on religion entirely and plunge into hedonism. The thing that can keep this from happening to your children is to give them spiritual direction while they are still young. Help your children to know and appreciate God's Word. Make sure they recognize that church is a necessary and *positive* part of every week. Sing with them, read the Bible with them, tell them the stories of Scripture, and make sure they spend time with other Christian kids. Cause them to desire God's will by praying together and asking the Lord to work in both small ways and large. These things will give spiritual direction to your children. Rather than telling them what Christians don't do, show them what Christians do.

Your kids should know how to read and use their Bibles. They should have some appropriate Scripture verses memorized that speak to their particular personalities. All of these things offer direction to a child. If you have a teen who is beginning to rebel, you can't jump in and offer guidance right away. You'll have to first make an effort to listen to your child, then speak with him a bit about his choices. If the relationship has been damaged, trust needs to be rebuilt before he'll be ready to listen to you offer him guidance. The best ways to earn that trust are to communicate and to set an example of First Chair faith.

That leads to the third need every child has: *a need for a spiritual model.* You son or daughter needs an example to follow. That's why sitting in the First Chair is so important; it reveals God's power through your life, rather than just through your words. Children very quickly pick up on the hypocrisy of the "do what I say, not what I do" style of parenting. Don't let your kids grow up thinking Christianity is mere words. Show them it's a way of living. Tell them what God has done for you. Give them an experience in the First Chair.

A model offers a pattern to follow. Most of us prefer to follow the example of another, rather than to create something entirely new. When you show your kids how you read Scripture, how you pray, and how you spend time listening to the Lord, you give them a model to try out. Every great spiritual teacher has had a few followers, and plenty of phony ones have gathered disciples around them. The Lord has given you a unique opportunity to model your experience of the First Chair for your kids; so put it to use.

The fourth spiritual need of your kids is that *they need a spiritual mentor.* This is different from a model. The model is the person who sets the example; the mentor is the person to whom they look for help. A spiritual mentor brings wisdom and encouragement to your child, offering advice and answering questions about spiritual things. The mentor has spiritual maturity, so he or she has something significant to share with your child.

You might be the spiritual mentor to your kids, or it might be someone else. Don't be afraid of a youth pastor or Sunday school leader being a spiritual mentor to your child. Often times they need the opportunity to ask questions of someone outside the family. Everybody needs someone like that to whom they can go. Make sure there is a spiritual mentor in the life of your child, so that someone can fill in the gaps of his faith.

NURTURING THE PEOPLE OF GOD

Your kids aren't just yours. They belong to God, and He has put them into your care. He expects you to nurture them so that you bring them up in the ways of God. If you are going to raise kids who love God and follow Him, there are six characteristics on which you need to focus.

First, *help them to know love*. I've already said quite a bit about this, but I must reiterate the importance of your children knowing they are loved if they are to love anyone else.

Second, *build their self-esteem*. A good self-image is perhaps the single most important tool for successfully facing the crises of life. It's the key to understanding the way your child treats others. We live in a culture that is experiencing an epidemic of inferiority, in the words of Dr. James Dobson, and your child's self-esteem isn't going to be enhanced by schools, friends, or the culture. So offer your kids plenty of praise. Look for good things to say about them. Help them find things they are good at, and do things that make them feel special. Let them know you'll always be there for them. Set realistic expectations for your kids, and keep on believing in them.

Third, *keep talking to them*. Your kids are inundated with messages that oppose God's values. They need your input. If you have any hope of offering them a First Chair experience with God, you've got to continue the communication. I've known fathers who have not communicated with their kids for years. Keep reminding your children that you love them, and keep listening to what they have to say so that you'll understand what they're going through. Look for good times to talk. Don't criticize, don't assume you know how they feel, and understand that good communication takes time.

Fourth, if you're going to nurture your kids, *build godly values into their lives*. They need to know the importance of integrity, how to overcome disappointment, and how Christians treat others. They need to see those values in your life.

Fifth, *learn to discipline in love*. The purpose of discipline is to shape your child's character, not just make life convenient for you. So establish some fair rules, be consistent in enforcing them, and learn to say things under control. Make sure to pay attention to your children's good behavior, so that they hear you say something besides correction all the time. When you do correct them, condemn the behavior and not the child. And learn to forgive them for their mistakes.

Finally, *make sure to introduce your children to the Lord*. Give them plenty of experience in the First Chair. That will nurture their spiritual lives. Your marriage can make a significant difference in the lives of your kids by nurturing them for the Lord.

MAKING A DIFFERENCE IN THE LIVES OF YOUR CHILDREN

Darlene and I didn't want our kids to just attend church. We wanted our kids to love Jesus. We wanted our marriage to reflect our own love for God and our commitment to Him. So we tried to reflect God's love. Our plan was to love them in the same way God loves them. To be honest, I failed way too often. But my kids grew to understand forgiveness, so they allowed me some failures. And they came to understand that loving Jesus Christ is the most important thing in life.

Your marriage can accomplish a tremendous amount in the lives of your children. Learn to enjoy them, whatever age they are.

Fathers, make an effort to enjoy your babies. Many fathers leave all the infant care up to the mothers, expecting to step in at an older age. But if the father doesn't take time to enjoy the baby, the child will soon learn that Dad is just there to hold things together when Mom is gone rather than being the leader of the house and someone with whom they should have a relationship. You can't begin your relationship with your kids when they are teenagers. If you lay the groundwork when they are small, you've got a solid foundation for building a healthy mature relationship when they are older.

If you are the parents of teens, I urge you to take all the time needed to build a bridge of communication to them. They need somebody who will listen to them and not criticize, somebody who will show them that he really cares. They need encouragement in their Christian walks, and they need to know for certain that they can count on you to be there for them when their plans fall apart. Set clear limits and discipline fairly, but allow them some freedom. Teens need to test out their wings! Show them that you trust them.

If you're not a patient person, you're going to have to develop the spiritual discipline of patience to parent teenagers. They need some understanding, and they require a lot of affirmation. More than anything, however, they need to know that their home is filled with love. If a teenager knows his parents are in love and will not divorce, they have significantly more confidence in facing the other troubling issues that are sure to arise. Teens want a happy home life. Your marriage can significantly change the life of a teen just by displaying your love for one another.

If showing love is the most important aspect in a home, spending time runs a close second. Our society is filled with couples who drop their kids off in the morning, then pick them up at night just in time to drop them in their beds so they can start the whole routine over again the next day. Love is often spelled "t-i-m-e" to children, and your time with your kids is limited. The worries and pressures of your life will always be there for you, but your children won't. If you want to make a big impact on their lives, spend a lot of time with them. I've spent time with a number of older men in the church. Many of them say that they wished they had spent more time with their kids. I've never yet heard a man say he wished he'd spent more time at the office.

Our lives are filled with activities. It seems as though every Christian family has meetings going on all week. Choir practice one night, a small group Bible study the next, a church committee meeting the following night, and prayer meeting yet another. Then there are the kids' sports programs, meetings for work, social gatherings with friends, and all the ministry meetings the church offers. With all that going on, who has time to spend just talking with their kids?

Overactivity is the bane of the modern Christian family. It robs us of time with one another. It pulls us apart, rather than pushing us together as a family. You must take control of your schedule by cutting back. Say "no" to some good things. Refuse to let your children participate in everything just because "everybody else is doing it." Turn off the television. Make time to spend with one another. It might be awkward at first, but you'll learn to love it. I'm convinced you just can't spend too much time with your family. And the best thing is that once you get into the habit of spending time together, you can't break it. If you establish the pattern when the children are young, then when they get older they will ask *you* to get together—an almost unthinkable proposition in many families these days.

What can your marriage accomplish? It sets the tone for the atmosphere in the entire family. It can change the lives of your children. It can allow them to see the importance of sitting in the First Chair with God and allowing His power to work in your life.

PASSING ON THE FAITH

Every Christian parent knows the importance of having his children make a decision for Christ. Your heart's desire is that each of your kids has a vibrant and growing relationship with God. Just thinking about one of your kids rejecting Jesus Christ is heartbreaking. Perhaps you've seen other parents anguish over their rebellious sons and daughters. You might have watched kids you grew up with in Sunday school leave the faith, bringing pain both to themselves and their parents. Research suggests that 70 percent of teens involved in a youth group will have stopped attending church within two years of their high school graduation. It's a devastating problem for parents and for the church.

The fact is, there are no sure-fire guarantees about raising kids. There is no method for training them that will absolutely assure you they will abide in the faith. Each man and woman must choose whom he or she will follow, and as hard as it may be to accept, some will reject Christ to follow their own selfish desires. We have to trust in the sovereign will of a loving God. He alone can save our children. Parents are called to obey the principles of faith development that have been revealed in His Word. We are called to trust the Lord to keep His promises. We know from His past dealings with mankind that He is a promise-keeping God.

On the day of Pentecost, the apostle Peter told the crowds, "Repent and be baptized, every one of you, in the name of Jesus Christ so that your sins may be forgiven. And you will receive the gift of the Holy Spirit. *The promise is for you and your children and for all who are far off*—for all whom the Lord our God will call" (Acts 2:38-39). God delights in saving the children of believers, but they are not brought to a saving faith automatically simply because of their parents' faith. They must be called, and they must decide to follow that calling. Thus the responsibility of the parents is to proclaim the Gospel to their children.

FAMILY DISCIPLESHIP

Have you ever heard a pastor read Deuteronomy Chapter 6 and wondered how it's supposed to look in practice? You know that great passage, "These are the commands, decrees and laws the Lord your God directed me to teach you to observe...so that you, your children, and their children after them may fear the Lord your God as long as you live by keeping all His decrees and commands that I give you, and so that you may enjoy long live" (Deuteronomy 6:1-2). We've heard that passage a thousand times; we even discussed it in the book. We know the verses that come next, too—the passage that teaches us to talk about Scripture with our kids and hang them on our walls. But many of us feel frustrated because we don't know how to put that passage in practice. "I know I'm supposed to be teaching the kids, and I know they need more from me, but I don't know how to do it. Maybe I don't have what it takes." Nobody enjoys feeling like a spiritual failure.

Over the years we've had some couples ask us how we discipled our kids. My wife likes to tell them that we always kept discipling a secret—we never let our kids know it was happening! Well, that's not always true. There were plenty of times when we had a formal devotional time as a family, but discipling our children consisted of much more than those times. Some Christians seem to think that unless the family is sitting quietly in a circle with Dad reading from a big Bible while the kids sit in rapt attention, they aren't "doing devotions." The truth is, you rarely get all your kids sitting quietly at once, unless they're watching the latest Star Trek movie. So we tried to think in terms of discipling our children rather than setting up a special devotional time. That way, each day brings several opportunities for training our children in the Lord.

All parents claim that they want to bring their children up "in the nurture and admonition of the Lord," but few have a plan for doing so. Few can name the values they want to build into the lives of their kids, and fewer still have developed a method for instilling those values. You see, the very first thing that must happen is that *you must claim the responsibility for discipling your children.* Not the youth leader, not the Sunday school teacher, not the Awana director. You. The church can't do in one or two hours what the parents have all week to accomplish. Set that in your mind as the first step. You will disciple your kids.

That will mean you and your spouse have to sit down with a paper and pencil, and think through exactly what your kids need in order to be learning and growing in their spiritual lives. What are the values you want to build into them? What do you want them to believe in? What are the most important things to you, and how do those translate to your children? *Writing these thoughts down on paper will allow you to mold your child, rather than waiting for the world mold him.* There is an old saying that goes, "If you don't know where you're going, chances are you'll end up somewhere else!"

You need a vision for what the "finished project" will look like. A builder doesn't just start nailing boards together; he draws a detailed picture of the house so that he knows what he is doing. Think about the character qualities you'd like in your children. You might have eighty things on your list at the start, but at that rate you'll still be working with your kids when you're on Social Security! You probably want to focus on a few things each year. For example, maybe this year you hope to convey the importance of honesty, trustworthiness, and self-control. Next year you can emphasize loving others, being kind, and being courteous.

The next logical question is, *"What steps do we need to take to produce that kind of person?"* You follow up your ideas with a specific strategy. Otherwise, you'd have a goal but no way of attaining it. Sit down as a couple and brainstorm some things you could do to build those qualities into your family. This isn't nearly as hard as it may seem at first. Choose a character trait like "obedience," find some Bible stories that illustrate it, like Noah, Abraham, and Gideon. Everybody loves stories, and we all like hearing about people. Find ways to work discussions of those people into your week. Then, a couple of times each month, think of some activities that would support the trait you're working on. For example, if you are working on obedience, you can focus on family chores, play "Simon Says," talk about Joshua's army, or tell stories about times you were disobedient.

I don't think you have to talk about these activities as devotions. You just have to make sure you have some sort of plan for moving your children ahead in their spiritual walks. Let's face it, taking the time to play hide-and-seek or wrestle with your kids can be a discipling activity. *As long as you reveal your life to them, show them what life is like in the First Chair, you are doing the work of discipleship.*

THE BUILDING BLOCKS OF FAITH

There are eight important principles for building faith in your children. You can expect to rely on each of these at one time or another, though all of them have the same goal. They all reveal your relationship with God. You don't have to make a fancy time of "devotions" out of them, as long as you are openly sharing your Christian life with your kids. Talk about who God is and what He has done in your life. Talk about what He has said in His Word, and how He wants us to live. As you share your faith, you'll find these principles help communicate it in new ways.

Building Block #1: *Tell stories*. Kids love stories. Little kids love the same stories again and again, because stories help them understand their world. Stories explain things, create vistas, and shrink the world into pieces a child can understand. Read all kinds of things to your kids: the Bible, books, magazines, activity pages, picture books—anything that supports your faith. And don't stop reading to them when they learn how to read. Reading to school-age children brings a closeness and a shared worldview that is hard to get any other way. Have your kids read to you. Don't settle for easy-readers. Get into the *Chronicles of Narnia* and the *Little House on the Prairie* books. Read the Bible to them, and make sure they see you reading it on your own. And when they get older, *tell* them stories. Tell them about your family, your life, your childhood, your birth, the world, everything. There is a myth out there that children hate hearing their parents talk about their childhoods. Most kids love to hear about it. Remember, school-age kids need to know facts, and teens need to understand the concepts behind the facts. Stories can open up communication between parents and teens.

Building Block #2: *Share dinners*. Make it a priority to eat together every day. It will bond your family and give you a chance to stay in contact with each other, which isn't easy anymore. We try to fill up our meal times with conversation: jokes, stories, what we're learning, the list is endless. I heard that Rose Kennedy used to write a topic on a chalkboard every day, and at the evening meal everyone was expected to be prepared to discuss it. She turned out a bunch of kids who knew their world.

Building Block #3: *Pray together*. Your children need to know how they can talk to God. If they see and hear you pray, they'll learn how. We used all kinds of things to help us pray: picture, lists, notebooks, prayer projects, letters from missionaries, you name it. We prayed for all sorts of things, at various times, and in all kinds of positions, so that the children could come to an understanding that prayer is simply talking to God. Help your kids see that God isn't some impersonal being "out there," but that He is a personal being who lives in your home with you. We reverence Him, but we can go to Him and talk at any time.

It's important that you pray for something that will allow the children to see God's power in action. As Evelyn Blitchington once said, "If God is not a prayer-answering God, aren't we better to find it out right now and have done with this pious nonsense? If God can't be approached with our everyday needs, aren't we better off to discover it right now, so that our children can be spared the hypocrisy and futility of believing in an all-powerful God who never lifts a finger?" Pray with your kids for God to use His power in important ways.

Building Block #4: *Memorize Scripture.* Memorizing verses is important because it is through that process that children learn the Word of God. The Bible makes a number of promises about itself—that those who memorize it will find guidance, growth, and a safeguard from sin. Those are things we all want our children to have. Take a passage and put it on the refrigerator, in lunch sacks, in the bathroom, or anywhere else that will help you remember it. When your child is struggling with a particular issue, memorize verses with her that speak directly to her problem. If you really want your child to be able to hear the thoughts of God, memorize with them. The keys are to repeat, review, and reinforce the verses regularly.

Building Block #5: *Use music.* Music is a great aid to family discipleship. For young children, listen to the Maranatha Kids, the Donut Man, and the "G.T. and the Halo Express" tapes. As they get older, buy them recordings of Christian artists who sing about the values important to your faith. Filling your home with music is both biblical and enjoyable. You might not be terribly musical, but a family that sings together will discover a great bonding that occurs through music.

Building Block #6: *Share hospitality.* Your children need to be exposed to other people, other cultures, and other ideas. Let them meet other Christians around your table and hear tales of what God has done in people's lives. Invite visiting missionaries over so that your children can get excited about what God is doing around the world. Hospitality also displays to your children the importance of caring for others, which is an essential part of the mature Christian's life.

Building Block #7: *Spend time.* It seems like we keep coming back to this point. Our lives are awfully busy, but too many parents become so busy they don't even parent their children. Use down time to do things together. Washing the car together is a great time to talk. Helping to sort laundry or going to the supermarket is a discipling activity because it allows your child to see how a mature Christian lives in the world. You won't be perfect, but that that's OK—it will allow your kids to see how to handle both success and failure. Wouldn't you rather they learned to live from watching you than from watching the tube? There's no substitute for spending time with your kids.

Please don't misunderstand what I'm saying. Not all your time together has to be filled with teaching. Make sure your kids know that you love them, and make sure they *feel* loved. Touch them, hold them, and take the time to listen to them. If you are living a godly life, they will catch a lot of it.

Building Block #8: *Model the Christian life.* If you are sitting in the First Chair, you know what the Lord is like. Share that with your kids. Most parents will never do that, either because they are too busy or too undisciplined. It takes strong commitment to disciple your children. In essence, you are telling the world that your children are more important than your other commitments. Children take precedence over committees. It will require you to slow the pace of your life considerably. You've got a lifetime to work at your job, but just a few short years to shape your children.

PRINCIPLES FOR PARENTS

I encourage every parent to take active steps to protect your children from Satan. Show them what it means to be *in* the world but not *of* the world. A list of do's and don'ts will never help your children deal with the lure of the world. They need to see how God's power works, and why it is a better choice than sin. Face it, you cannot make your teenager's decisions for him. Don't think you have to protect them from the struggle of deciding—struggle is necessary if they are to develop character and responsibility. It's my view that the "Christians Don't Do This" type of parenting prevents their character from developing and retards their growth.

Having said that, I recognize that the number one reason young people fall away from the faith is because they enjoy the lure of the world's temptations. To a young person who has never personally experienced the power of God, sin can look appealing compared to "the boring old rules of the Christian life." It's your job to help your child view life through the spectacles of God's Word. You're going to have to acquaint him with the philosophy and lifestyle of the world, but at the same time you're going to be ready to reveal why the Christian life is a superior alternative. You see, Christians are not of this world. This world is Satan's domain. It is lost and destined for destruction. Our citizenship, according to Philippians 3:20, is in heaven. We have a new nature and a new responsibility. We seek the kingdom of God, rather than the pleasures of this world. Your kids need to see you demonstrate that attitude by your lifestyle. You need to show them that being a Christian is not a matter of do's and don'ts, but that it is a matter of the affection of your heart. Everyone on earth is either seeking their own pleasure or seeking to please God.

Carl Spackman, a Pennsylvania pastor, once said, "Our children need to know that God made this world as a place to be viewed as good, to be received with thanksgiving, and to be a blessing to mankind. But they must also be told that, in its fallen condition, it has become a world in rebellion against its Creator. Sinful men have taken the things of this world and used them for their own selfish and lustful ends instead of as a means of praising God. Christians, however, are to be different in their attitude toward the world. The problem is many of us are not that much different."

I've known Christians who won't go to the movie theater, but rent R-rated movies to watch on their home VCRs. I know people who criticize popular fiction being used in high school English classes, but read those very same books at home. That sort of hypocrisy will kill the faith of your children. There's an alarming tendency for Christians to accommodate the world's standards, but Romans 12 warns us to not allow the world to "squeeze us into its mold." We've got to be different. We've got to be holy. We've got to know how Satan works and how to resist him. And we've got to pass that knowledge on to our kids.

You see, setting an example is only half the battle. You must set a *holy* example in your home, at your job, in your car—everywhere you go, Jesus is with you. Let your children see that you are the same person at the ball game on Friday night that you are in church on Sunday morning.

The other part of the job is to actively seek ways to share your faith with your kids. Help them crawl into your lap as you sit in that First Chair, so that they not only *see* you living the Christian life, they experience God's power. You've got to help them have an emotional response to the power of God. You've got to help them see God work in your life and in their lives. Then they'll appreciate what God can do, and why they need to commit to Him. When they see Christ as being superior to the world, they'll want that for themselves.

WHEN YOUR CHILDREN MAKE BAD CHOICES

"Train up a child in the way he should go, and when he is old he will not depart from it," Solomon tells us in Proverbs 22:6. Many parents have claimed that as a promise, to the disappointment and chagrin of others. If your children grew up and never made a decision for Christ, you probably feel as though the Lord let you down.

Parents, the Proverbs convey divinely inspired observations about the world. They tell truth about what normally happens, giving insight into the affairs of men. But you are not to lift one verse out and make it stand as a guarantee. The Proverbs tell what normally will occur in a situation. They refer to probabilities, if you will, not promises of God. For example, Proverbs 10:4 says that "lazy hands make a man poor, but diligent hands brings wealth." But we have all heard of lazy men who stumbled into a business gold mine, and most of us have known diligent workers who lost everything in a crash or because of an illness. The Proverbs aren't given to us as ironclad guarantees, but as observations about life.

Adam's father was the Lord Himself. God certainly loved Adam, and He "raised" Adam the way he should be raised. Yet Adam sinned and strayed from God. A literal reading of Proverbs 22:6 would implicate God in a major theological conundrum! The fact is, sometimes godly parents have rebellious kids.

I start with that verse in Proverbs because I want to talk to parents who are hurting. Churches are full of mothers and fathers who ache deeply because of the choices their children have made. We hate the fact that our kids make lousy choices sometimes, and when they make a life-changing choice that is bad we are pained to the core of our beings.

PAINFUL PARENTING

A friend of mine and his wife did everything for their son that they could; they gave him every advantage. He might have been a bit spoiled when he was young, but for the most part he was an obedient child. Then he hit his teen years and everything fell apart. He barked at his mom, was sullen with his dad, and started hanging around with a pretty coarse group of kids. He began using drugs and alcohol, got his girlfriend pregnant, and dropped out of high school his junior year. They tried all sorts of interventions, to no avail. The kid didn't want help, and he didn't want to change. Eventually he moved in with his girlfriend, then dropped out of their lives completely. His parents have heard he has a serious drug problem, and is on public assistance.

The pain this couple has gone through is heartbreaking. They changed churches so they wouldn't have to face people asking about their boy. For a while they even talked about leaving the church entirely. God hadn't been faithful, they said, though at heart they really thought it was all their fault. They've both suffered serious depression. It wouldn't surprise me if the mother has been suicidal at times. And it's all because of the choices their son made.

We have known couples who have been overwhelmed with guilt over the actions of their kids. I've known men who left the ministry because they no longer felt qualified to talk to parents about raising children.

If you are suffering from the choices of your children, my heart goes out to you. It's easy to feel insecure when your kids have rejected the faith. It's easy to lose confidence in yourself and in your role as a parent. Even if you have other children who turned out just fine, you can kick yourself for the one who didn't. Nothing makes a parent feel like a failure more than watching a son or daughter foul up his or her life. The guilt stays with you. You feel that you are responsible, and you might be completely overwhelmed. At least one mother I've known spent two weeks just sitting at her kitchen table after she found out her unmarried daughter was pregnant and living with her boyfriend. She couldn't talk about it, she couldn't take care of anything—she just sat in shock, staring out the window and thinking about her pain.

Most of us probably never realized the potential for pain having children brings. When your daughter was born, you looked at that little life, totally dependent upon you for everything, and you were amazed at the miracle of birth. Your heart was so filled with love you thought it would burst. You poured your life into her, desiring only the best to come her way. How she moved from being a dependent little angel to being an independent woman causing you heartache is a mystery.

Our kids can cause us incredible joy and incredible sorrow. We want to see them succeed. We hate to see them fail. Perhaps we hate worse seeing our own bad habits mirrored in their lives. The world offers a myriad of dangerous inducements to our children. We want them to say no to the world, and to choose to live for God. We want them to sit in the First Chair with the Lord Jesus Christ. But sometimes they don't.

Dr. James Dobson found that 21 percent of all kids can be considered "strong-willed" from the time they are little. These kids are much more likely to rebel against parental authority, struggle with school, and depend on their peer group for approval. Nearly every child goes through a few tough times in his teens, but most strong-willed children experience significant rebellion. The parents of these kids blame themselves. They think about the things they could have done differently. They are embarrassed at the behavior of their children, and ashamed of their parenting job. And, in case you are wondering, *this even happens to the children of First Chair parents*.

It's possible to sit in the First Chair, share the power of God with your child, and still have him reject Jesus Christ. While you have been given the responsibility to share the love and the truth of God with him, each person is ultimately responsible for his or her own choices. There is a dominant theory of psychology called "determinism," that claims all children are born completely neutral. If they turn out badly, according to that school of thought, it's because the child's situation was bad. The family, the culture, and most important *the parents* made terrible mistakes raising the child. I talk to parents on a regular basis who are living with guilt because their adult children aren't walking with the Lord, and they blame themselves. They think that they could have altered a few situations, acted differently to their children, and somehow things would have worked out entirely different. They listen to people who have been influenced by the writings of B. F. Skinner, and accept the behaviorist notion that you can turn out a child exactly how you desire simply by changing the programming you offer him. This sort of thinking has become all the rage, to the point that criminals are claiming they aren't to be held responsible for their actions—their parents are to blame!

The problem with this thinking is that it is thoroughly unbiblical. Children aren't born neutral, nor are they born as innocent little angels. Everyone, according to the Bible, is born dead in his sins. If you take a child and give her absolutely no direction, will she turn out to be a charming young lady? No, she'll turn out a selfish, spoiled brat. So I can't figure out why so many Christians have bought into the concepts of determinism or behaviorism. If you accept these theories as truth, then every problem a child experiences is really the fault of the parents. It's my contention that parents are too willing to blame themselves for everything bad their kids do—and particularly everything their adolescents do.

That is a fairly recent phenomenon. It used to be assumed that if a child acted badly, it was because he was a bad kid. Now we want to blame the parents for everything, and that's wrong. Certainly there are parents who warp their children. Sexual and emotional abuse or parental neglect can damage a child's life and psyche. There aren't any prerequisites to being a parent, so there are plenty of people who have had children before they were ready for the responsibility. Those kids who were raised in bad homes have a tendency to pass on those behaviors, because when they grow up they don't have any other idea how to parent. But I've known people who care for their sons and daughters deeply, do their best to live in the First Chair, and still watch as their children entangle themselves in sin. We've watched loving parents fall to pieces because their teenager turned surly, rejected the faith, and began getting involved in all sorts of wickedness. It's one of the most devastating experiences possible for a parent. It can shake his or her faith in God. It can damage their marriage. It can make them wish their child was dead rather than be involved in such heinous activity. And the parents will blame themselves.

You know, I don't believe the parents of a bad kid necessarily need to take all the blame. There is no proof that you have ruined your son's life just because he isn't walking with the Lord. Guilt is a funny thing. It stays with you; a painful emotion that's hard to live down. Sometimes it can be God's sign of displeasure, but at other times it can be our own creation, or perhaps the creation of Satan trying to get you to take blame for things that are not your fault. For example, we know a family that has three kids who absolutely love the Lord Jesus Christ, and one son who lives as a total reprobate. If they are such bad parents, why did the other three turn out so well? I think much of the difference between the kids is due to their temperaments and their own choices rather than the failures and weaknesses of the parents.

As a parent, I am flawed. I'm not perfect, so I can't expect to always make the right choices. There have been times I've blown it with my kids, and many more times that I've had to *guess* at what was right because I really didn't know. Sometimes my errors in judgment have caused problems. Sometimes my own selfishness got in the way. I made mistakes, but the truth is everybody makes some mistakes in parenting. You simply cannot assume that every bad choice your kids make is because of your own mistakes.

This is a hard thing to say, because I don't want readers to think that I'm absolving all parents of blame. I believe that it is the parents' job to do the best they can to raise their kids, and to share with their children the spiritual experience of the First Chair. I further believe that many Christian parents don't adequately do that because of their own Second Chair faith. Hence, their children end up sitting in the Third Chair and rejecting God. However, parents have to remember that children grow into accountable adults, and every adult is responsible for his own choices.

Not long ago I spoke with a pastor who was considering leaving the ministry because of his son's sexually illicit behavior. He felt that Paul's letter to Timothy describing the qualifications for eldership made it clear he was unqualified to pastor. But that man's son was in his twenties! The passage concerning eldership is talking about children. In Paul's day most people were married by age fourteen or fifteen. The apostle was warning against offering a leadership position to a man whose family is in chaos, not a man who watches his mature son rebel against God. Adults are responsible for their own choices.

The prophet Ezekiel warned about this very problem: "The soul who sins is the one who will die. The son will not share the guilt of the father, *nor will the father share the guilt of the son.* The righteousness of the righteous man will be credited to him, and the wickedness of the wicked will be charged against him" (Ezekiel 18:20).

You need to be praying for your children. You need to be nurturing them in the Lord by sharing your spiritual life with them You need to create a trusting, positive environment, offering encouragement and wisdom, and talking with them about what is happening in their lives. But recognize that your child will grow to be a man or woman who is responsible and answerable to God.

SEASONS OF A FAMILY

One of the best things you can do to see your family through difficult times is to pray. Pray for God to protect them. Pray for the Spirit to make them strong. Pray for the Lord to place significant individuals in their lives who can influence them. And don't stop praying just because they make some mistakes or walk away from the Lord. Keep praying for the "hound of heaven" to be in hot pursuit in the life of your child.

All families go through seasons—periods of time that are similar for every family, and in which we can identify certain characteristics.

First, there is *the season of infants.* At this time parents need to build trust into the lives of their kids and make them feel loved. A child who knows she is cared for can more easily trust a loving God when she is older. A child who sees significant investment in his life by both parents understands the important role they play. A child who is encouraged to take some initiative begins to develop a healthy self-image. And, as I said, fathers need to be involved at this stage just as much as mothers do. If you think you'll jump into the mix when the child is in school, you're wrong. That will be too late. Learn to enjoy parenting the littlest ones.

Next come *the season of children.* During this time the parents need to set clear rules and live by them consistently. This is the time when you tell your children the stories of Jesus, pray with them, and let them see the example you set as a Christian. Talk with them about the issues in their lives. Let them know that you are the authority, but approach them with a sense of humor. The central issue a parent faces is normally the problem of power. Your kids will want to test the limits of power when it comes to bedtime, mealtime, homework, and obedience. If you are firm but fair in the beginning, your family will often develop a healthy pattern. If you appease their power struggle, you'll be headed down the path toward heartache.

The third season is the hardest for nearly every parent: *the season of teens.* Educators will tell you that when a child reaches the age of twelve or thirteen, something significant happens in their reasoning abilities. Rather than simply dealing with concrete issues, the junior high-aged student can begin to reason in the abstract. He can begin to think about the ideal. And that allows him to see that his parents are somewhat less than ideal. He begins arguing over little things, becomes sensitive over the slightest matter, and is alternately excited and sullen. Once they can reason, they can become unreasonable!

These troubles are a combination of physiological and social changes. Their hormones are changing, causing mood swings and emotional changes. Their peer group is becoming more important, so that acceptance by others is the ultimate goal of the child between the ages of fourteen and sixteen years old. Beauty becomes the most important characteristic of girls, and athletic success the most important for boys. Unfortunately, there are few really beautiful or athletically gifted fifteen-year-olds, so the peer group at school forms a sort of hierarchy. There are emotional dangers lurking to trap your son or daughter at nearly every turn.

With this sort of scary stuff happening, I'd like to make a couple suggestions to parents of teens. Remember to pray much for your children. Make efforts to communicate positively with them, and spend much more time listening than talking. Fathers, I encourage you to sit on the bed of your child every night and just listen to what they have to say. (Be patient, it might take them twenty minutes or so to get there!) Reveal your spiritual walk to them, so that they have a model to follow.

Another important principle is to keep your teenager busy. Get her involved in the youth group. Help him go on the short-term missions trip from church. They may be tough to get up in the morning, but most teens have energy to burn once they're up. If your church doesn't have a solid youth ministry, consider pretty carefully if you want to keep attending there, especially if your child is prone to finding mischief. A busy kid can't get into as much trouble as a kid with time on his hands.

Your teenager needs your attention and your time. He needs to know that you care for him and are there for him. Your daughter needs to feel that you care about her enough to spend time with her. That may mean cutting back on your schedule, but the teen years will only happen once (thank heavens!).

Charles Stanley talks about "keeping your teens on your team." In other words, go easy on them. Don't look for fights; pick your spots carefully. Your teens will be in the process of deciding how they will be different from you. Let them make some choices that you wouldn't make, like in music or clothes. Of course, I can't condone much of the filth-filled rock music on the radio or the shirts plastered with inappropriate phrases, but neither do they have to listen to the oldies station and wear white shirts with ties. Try to keep three things in mind when you've got a teenager. First, *let them choose*. As much as possible, allow them to make their own choices. Why fight about the small stuff? As they become adults they are going to have to learn how to make good choices anyway. Second, *let them fail*. Your first inclination will be to save your child every time they make a lousy choice. Unless it's dangerous and sinful, try to stay out of it. Remember, experience is the best teacher. Third, *let them go*. Don't expect your teen to act the same way she did as a child. Let them do some things differently. They'll appreciate you treating them like adults, rather than children. Dads, cultivate some common interests with your kids. Moms, give them as many encouraging remarks as possible. Keep your marriage healthy, remain close to God, and keep talking with your kids about life.

Nothing will make more of an impact on a confused young person than those three things.

This third season is by far the hardest. There are changes in your kids you never dreamed of, but if you can keep it low-key, keep them on your side, keep talking, and above all keep praying, you'll survive it all.

The next season in your family is *the young adult season*. This is generally where parents can take a deep breath. The turbulent teen years have passed, and your kids have begun making more permanent decisions about their lives. Parents are often amazed at the calmness in the family after the years of uproar. If you've kept the communication lines open, this can be a wonderful time of sharing wisdom and watching your children take off. All those times you shared your spiritual life with your children will be evidenced as they make their faith their own.

The next season is *the adult season*, when you get to smile at your kids going through all the same headaches you went through! Many a parent has enjoyed listening to his adult child complain about teens not listening, figuring that "what goes around comes around." Now you get to pray for the faith of your grandkids to be as vibrant as your own.

LIVING WITH DISASTER

Unfortunately, things don't always work out the way we want them to. Our kids can grow up to make bad choices, regardless of how well you parent. You'll feel deep pain, for no one likes to see a loved one hurt. But in the midst of your pain, keep some things in mind. First, remember that Christ loves you and has called you to Himself. Your faith can be severely shaken by a son or daughter who openly rejects Jesus Christ. Allow yourself some time to grieve, but keep yourself close to Christ. Read your Bible every day. Pour out your heart to God in your quiet time. Let Him know how badly you hurt, and He can minister to you. Find a close brother or sister in Christ with whom you can vent your frustrations and who can support you in prayer. The worst thing for your child will be for *you* to give up on Christ, too.

Second, keep praying. My folks prayed for years that one of my siblings would return to Jesus Christ. It took a long time, but it finally happened. Remember, the thief on the cross was a terrible disappointment to a mother somewhere, but in the end he turned to God. Our Lord is still in the business of changing lives, even lives that have been wallowing in sin and selfishness for years. Keep your faith in a forgiving God who still loves your child and has the power to change him.

Third, cleave to your mate. Many times when a child goes into rebellion, the father clams up and the mother becomes bitter. Don't let your child's bad choices ruin your marriage. Talk about it. If you need help talking about it, go together to talk with your pastor or a Christian counselor. Keep the communication going. If it breaks down, you'll be facing your pain alone rather than with your God-given partner. Being alone in that devastating pain is far worse than talking about it with someone who understands like no other—your spouse.

Finally, remain in the First Chair. If your children have experienced the power of God in your life, it will stay with them forever. They might try to run away from God, but inside they know that what you have is truth and all else is falsehood. Your First Chair relationship can still make a significant impact, even years after they've experienced it.

Living in the First Chair isn't easy. It will require commitment, submission, and a total reliance on God. But if you do it, if you allow the power of God to change your life and you help your children to share your experience, you'll have gone a long toward making sure your kids sit in that First Chair. You'll have begun a legacy that can live on for generations.

STUDY QUESTIONS

1. How do you show love to your children?

2. What steps would you like to take to begin discipling your children better?

3. Where do parents find solace when their children are in rebellion to the Lord?

4. Which chair are you sitting in?

5. What will it take to get you to move to the First Chair?